BLESSING FROM AGNES

Susan Urbanek Linville

For permission, serialization, condensation, adaptions, or for our catalog of other publications, write to Ozark Mountain Publishing, Inc., P.O. Box 754, Huntsville, AR 72740, ATTN: Permissions Department.

Library of Congress Cataloging-in-Publication Data

Blessing from Agnes by Susan Urbanek Linville -1956-

True events that interweaves the struggles of the early Spiritualists and Karen's efforts to remain "normal" in an old western Pennsylvania steel town.

1. Near Death Experience 2. Medium 3. Spiritualism 4. Grief

I. Susan Urbanek Linville, 1956 II. Spiritualism III. Metaphysical IV. Title

Library of Congress Catalog Card Number: 2022942878

ISBN: 9781950639168

Cover Art and Layout: Victoria Cooper Art

Book set in: Multiple Fonts

Book Design: Summer Garr

Published by:

PO Box 754, Huntsville, AR 72740

800-935-0045 or 479-738-2348; fax 479-738-2448

WWW.OZARKMT.COM

Printed in the United States of America

"You will face many defeats in life, but never let yourself be defeated."
—Maya Angelou

CONTENTS

CHAPTER 1

1956: UNEXPECTED COMPLICATIONS

New Castle Hospital's children's floor was decorated with paper jack-o-lanterns, witches, and skeletons. With midnight approaching, the chatter of little voices, impatient cries, and whimpers gave way to silence. Mary Jean Oberleitner walked the length of the main corridor and stood at the window overlooking the side street. Just peeking over the rooftops of neighboring houses was the upper floor of the National Bank building several blocks away. All the lights were on. She imagined a cleaning woman busy vacuuming, dusting, and emptying trash cans. She would give anything right then to be occupied by mindless work instead of worrying about her daughter's health.

Mary stretched to get the kink out of her neck and strolled back toward her daughter's room. The door to the children's ward stood open. Some of the children slept soundly, others rested quietly. A black-haired boy with dark brown eyes near the door was restless, tapping his foot on the edge of the iron crib. She smiled at him, but he turned away with a shy grin. Her chest ached at the thought that the little tyke had to be left alone. She couldn't understand how parents could leave children that small in the hospital all night. She felt anxious leaving her daughter, Karen, alone even for a few minutes.

Mary continued along the hall to Karen's room. Karen had been a sickly child since birth and had been hospitalized at one year of age with a terrible fever. Mary was afraid they were going to lose her that night, but her daughter was a fighter. The fever broke toward morning.

Karen rolled to her side when Mary entered the room and peered through the rungs of the white iron crib.

"You are supposed to be sleeping," Mary said.

"I want a pumpkin," Karen said.

"We'll get a pumpkin, soon," Mary said. She couldn't believe October was half over and Halloween was quickly approaching. This October would be different from last year when Karen suffered with one of her persistent throat infections. With no tonsils, they could go trick-or-treating without worry. "Daddy can help you carve it."

Mary bent over the edge of the crib and brushed aside one of Karen's brown ringlets. The rail held a thick layer of white enamel with indentations of tiny teeth from children who been hospitalized here before. Mary knew her daughter was safe here; the hospital staff and doctors were almost like family. Still, she couldn't shake the pervasive fear of losing another child.

"I want to go home," Karen said. She was small for her age and looked even smaller in the white hospital gown and large bed. "It smells bad here."

"That's just disinfectant," Mary said. "We'll get those nasty tonsils out in the morning. After that, you can have some ice cream. Now, it's time for sleep."

"I don't want to do my tonsils," Karen said.

"Without tonsils you won't have sore throats. You'll like that, won't you?"

Karen nodded.

"The doctor will give you some special medicine to breathe," Mary said. "It will be over before you know it."

"Then we can have ice cream?"

"That's right. All the ice cream you want."

* * *

Mary didn't remember falling asleep in the chair. It was still dark outside when a young nurse entered the room. Mary didn't recognize her. She could have been Doris Day's twin, with the same upturned nose and big eyes, but she wore a little too much makeup for Mary's taste. Nurses should look professional, not like they were going out to the movies.

"You have to leave now, ma'am," the nurse said. "I need to get your daughter ready."

Mary assumed she was one of the new graduates. She resisted the urge to inform the young woman that she was a registered nurse and knew the protocol. But today she wasn't a nurse. She was a mother. She bent over and kissed Karen on the forehead.

"I want my ice cream," Karen said.

"Not yet," Mary said. "This nurse is going to take you to surgery. I'll see you when you're finished."

"No," Karen said, reaching for her. "I don't want you to go."

"I know," she said. "You be a good girl for the nurse. I'll see you soon."

Karen whined. Mary held her breath and forced herself to leave the room. It was best this way, even if her heart was screaming for her to stay and protect her only child. She focused on the corridor to the elevator. The same green tile lined every floor of the hospital. She couldn't count the times she'd walked identical halls during her years of nursing school.

The elevator dinged and the door slid open. She pushed the button for the surgical wing. Dr. Ginsburg had invited her into surgery, but she didn't want to put herself in a compromising situation. She'd be watching from the observation room. It was better that way.

Mary found a seat overlooking the surgical suite. The room was clean, green tile floor sparkling. Tools were already laid out on a tray next to the table. She'd been here many times as a nursing student and had watched several minor operations. She was one of the few students who didn't faint at their first sight of blood.

"It's just a minor procedure," Mary told herself. Everything was going to be fine.

Her sister had complained that Karen was too young for a

tonsillectomy. Four years of age was a bit young, but Karen's tonsils became so large with each infection, she would gasp for breath at night. Besides, modern medicine was working miracles. Drugs like penicillin and Terramycin were eliminating life-threatening infections. Streptomycin was being used to treat TB. Just two years before, surgeons had performed the first heart surgery with a heart-lung machine in Philadelphia. Tonsillectomies were routine. Everyone was getting them these days, adults and children alike.

Dr. Ginsburg carried Karen into the surgical suite. Her head was covered with a reddish cap, and a matching bib was tied around her neck. He sat her on the table. Mary clasped her hands in prayer. The doctor's familiar square chin and black glasses poised on his large nose was oddly comforting. He knew Mary had lost her firstborn infant daughter and miscarried her second pregnancy. He understood how special Karen was to her. He would be careful.

Dr. Newman, Karen's pediatrician, entered a few minutes later. By then, Karen was already relaxed from the Atropine injection. The assisting nurse handed the bottle of ether and filter mask to Dr. Ginsburg. A few breaths and Karen would sleep for the procedure. Her throat would be sore afterward, but she wouldn't feel any of the pain during surgery.

Dr. Ginsburg held the filter over Karen's nose and mouth. Drip. Drip. Her shoulders sagged. The doctor laid her back and said something to the nurse. The nurse handed him retractors. He inserted them between Karen's lips and opened her mouth. The nurse used forceps to pull her tongue out of the way. Karen's face looked pale.

The nurse handed the doctor a scalpel.

Karen's lips turned blue.

Blue. Blue meant no oxygen. Her lips shouldn't be blue.

Mary's heart raced. She tapped on the glass.

Dr. Ginsburg shoved the nurse aside and removed the retractor.

"No!" Mary heard herself yell. No. No. No.

The doctor massaged Karen's chest. He lifted her arms above

her head.

Mary's ears rang. This was supposed to be a routine procedure. What had she done?

Dr. Ginsburg dropped to the floor in a faint.

"Oh, my God in heaven," Mary said. She remembered her baby girl dying in her arms, the breath going out of her. "Hail Mary full of grace," she prayed. "The Lord is with thee. Blessed art thou among women, and blessed is the fruit of thy womb, Jesus. Holy Mary, mother of God, pray for us sinners now, and at the hour of death. Glory Be to the Father, and to the Son, and to the Holy Spirit."

"Get help," Dr. Newman snapped.

The nurse ran from the surgical suite. Dr. Newmark stepped around Dr. Ginsburg and worked Karen's arms toward her chest and back. He blew air into her mouth.

* * *

"Is it time for ice cream?"

Karen slid downward in a spiral like she was on a water ride at Cascade Park. Everything whirled. Around and around. But there wasn't any water, and there weren't any trees. Everything was dark.

"Momma?" Were those nasty tonsils out? She didn't think so.

Wooden boards twisted around her like in the *Wizard of Oz* movie when the tornado lifted Dorothy's house into the air. The boards flew like a flock of birds, only there wasn't any sky or trees or clouds. Everything beyond was gray.

This wasn't right. She wasn't in the hospital. She wasn't at home. She shouldn't be in this place. She was afraid.

"I want my momma!"

The boards vanished and everything went black. Dampness surrounded her. Walls felt close, like she stood in a long tunnel, but she couldn't see walls or floor or ceiling. She turned, but there was nothing behind her, nothing to her sides. No sound. No smell. She couldn't feel her hands or feet, but she felt herself moving through the darkness. Floating.

5

"I want to go home."

Light began as a small pinprick far in the distance. It bloomed, growing larger and brighter as she floated closer. Was that the window in her room? Momma would be there, waiting for her. They would go get ice cream. Everything would be okay.

A calming warmth soothed her. No, the light wasn't the window in her room. It wasn't the hospital. She was supposed to be here. This was a good place. She just needed to reach the light. Then everything would be okay.

No more nasty tonsils. No more fevers.

Almost there.

She just needed to go a bit further.

* * *

Karen smelled ether. Yuck. Her nose was cold. Her fingers were cold. She shivered.

Arms squeezed her tight. She blinked her eyes open. She tried to whisper, but her throat was dry and the words didn't come out.

"It's okay, sweetie," Momma said. "I have you now."

Karen leaned into her embrace. Momma. She was all right.

"You're safe here with me," Momma said.

"Safe," Karen rasped. Momma was right. Everything was going to be okay, but there was no light here. It had been so warm, so comforting. She wanted to stay with Momma and at the same time wanted to go back to the light.

"I'm not letting you go," Momma said.

No, Karen thought. She wasn't going back to the light. Her body was too cold and heavy now. The warm light was turned off, but she knew she would find it again someday.

CHAPTER 2

1907: FORTUNE-TELLER

The doorbell chimed, echoing up the steps of the two-story Victorian. Lydia Marquette had no scheduled appointments and didn't expect anyone on such a blustery March day. *In like a lamb and out like a lion.* She couldn't remember if that meant an early or late summer. By this point, she would be happy with any amount of warmth.

She grabbed her skirt and hiked it up above her ankles to descend the steep steps. The chime rang a second time.

"Coming," she said.

She steeled herself and opened the front door. Air laden with soot and dust gusted in from the porch, chilling her bones. Lydia struggled to breathe, then took slow and shallow breaths as the doctor had recommended for her condition. Her lungs did not like life in the dirty city, but what could she do? Her husband, Edward's, job dispatching for the Pennsylvania Railroad Company had brought them to New Castle two years ago. According to her spirit guide, Charley, they were here to stay.

A woman, at least twenty years Lydia's senior, wrapped in a fine black tweed coat with matching hat greeted her with a stern expression. "Are you the fortune-teller?"

"I am not a fortune-teller," Lydia said. "I am a *spiritual medium.*"

A motorcar raced along the brick street, belching over the din of the pounding steel mill, only a stone's throw along the opposite bank of Neshannock Creek. A horse hitched to a buggy out front of the IOOF hall whinnied.

"I do readings," Lydia continued. "I deliver messages from the dearly departed. I do not engage in psychic readings nor tell futures."

The woman glanced nervously over her shoulder, as if a husband or jealous lover might be watching.

"How much?" she said.

"I ask a small donation of fifty cents."

"All right then," the woman said.

Lydia stepped back. "Please, do come in."

The woman paused at the mirrored coat rack to remove her gloves and hat. Beneath her coat she donned a simple but tailored white blouse and gored skirt with matching jacket. Her gray-streaked brown hair was styled into a pompadour with psyche knot. She folded her gloves and slid them into the coat pocket, then hung the hat and coat on a peg.

"My reading room is upstairs," Lydia said. "Mrs.?"

"I'd rather not say."

"I understand." Or at least she tried to be insightful. She had assumed that when they moved to the "big city," people would be more worldly. But she had been wrong. The people of New Castle were just as backward as the folks in her hometown in Colorado. They put their own religion before any other, and assumed they had a complete understanding of God and the heavens. They refused to accept Spiritualism as anything but pagan rituals or devil worship, or some such nonsense.

"I shall call you Mrs. Jones then."

Lydia led Mrs. Jones up the carpeted stairs. The reading room was toward the front of the house, overlooking the street and creek. A small coal fire burned low in the fireplace, barely enough to keep out the chill of the day. Lydia motioned for Mrs. Jones to sit across a round card table in the center of the room covered with a plain linen cloth. Some mediums preferred extravagant trappings, imported mahogany tables, closets within which to focus the vibrations from the spiritual realm, crystal orbs or burning candles. Lydia chose simplicity.

Charley was all she needed. Her spirit guide seemed to be

extra cooperative since they'd moved to New Castle. When she'd asked him if he had a connection to the place, he'd said the river was like time, the same and ever changing. She hadn't understood him, but knew she also felt at peace with the river flowing so closely.

"Shall I pay you now?" Mrs. Jones brought forth a bead-encrusted change purse from her skirt pocket and placed it on the table.

"No," Lydia said. "You may leave a donation on the table after the reading."

"Whatever you say," Mrs. Jones said.

Lydia settled into her overstuffed floral chair. Morning light filtered through sheer curtains, casting opaque shadows across a divan and small bookcase on the opposite wall. Mrs. Jones fidgeted in an oak chair. She glanced about the neatly furnished room, gaze stopping on a photograph of Lydia's diseased mother. God rest her soul.

"I see no cards or crystals," Mrs. Jones said. "When does this begin? I don't have all day."

"As I have already stated," Lydia said, "I am not a fortune-teller. Sometimes future events come to light during my readings, but that is not my purpose."

Mrs. Jones tapped her foot. Lydia couldn't tell if it was impatience or nerves.

"I do have a guide who helps me," Lydia said.

"Guide?"

"Yes, his name is Charley," Lydia said. "Some mediums need no guidance, but I …"

"Then what does your guide have to say," she said, "about my future?"

Lydia breathed deeply. She had never pretended, hinted, published, nor advertised that she could read any person's future or possess a power beyond the understanding of mankind. It seemed that there were many clients of late who came visiting with such expectations. Mrs. Jones certainly was the most tenacious of those.

"I will need a moment to concentrate," Lydia said. And clear her mind of negative vibrations that this woman had brought with her. It was difficult enough to call Charley from beyond the veil when she was calm, but sometimes people made her so angry, she was unable to reach him at all. She breathed deeply, trying to cleanse her mind of all irate thoughts. The woman remained quiet. Lydia relaxed.

"Charley," she whispered in her mind. "Charley."

Lydia knocked on the table three times.

Charley's presence arrived as the scent of bitter almonds. Lydia saw him in her mind's eye as a young man with thick curly hair and dark eyes. He'd certainly been attractive in life, but his spirit was marked with a bluish aura that echoed a sadness. It was a sadness he'd never shared with her, despite her urging.

She is too judgmental, Charley said.

I can see that.

Then you also know I do not tolerate such persons.

Be patient, Charley, Lydia said. *She was brought to us for a reason.*

There were others in the shadows behind him, a woman and maybe a young boy, but they remained aloof. It was not unusual for a client's attitude to keep the spirits at bay. Lydia would try to coax them forward. She rubbed her palms together.

"There are two spirits here," Lydia said. "A woman. A mother or grandmother. And a child."

Mrs. Jones wants to hear none of this, Charley said.

Charley, please, pay attention and help me.

Bitter almond tickled her throat. Lydia coughed.

"Excuse me," she said. "My spirit guide is being stubborn today."

Mrs. Jones's change purse rattled. "I do not intend to pay if you cannot give me a fortune. I see that this was a mistake."

Lydia fought back her rising anger. She wanted to let the woman walk out but felt there was at least one spirit who was there to deliver a message. She reminded herself that she worked for the spirit world, they did not work for her.

"One moment," Lydia said. She worked to calm herself again.

Who are they, Charley?

The long forgotten, he said. By her and her husband. He *passes judgment on others despite the teaching of his so-called religion.*

"I see that you live alone with your husband in the city," Lydia said.

"That is incorrect," Mrs. Jones said.

One other, Charley said.

"I'm sorry," Lydia said. "Three. There are three of you in the home."

"That was a guess," Mrs. Jones said. "What kind of fortune-teller are you?"

Lydia's cheeks warmed.

Tell her there will be a death in the family, said Charley. *See what she says to that.*

"Please don't be alarmed," Lydia said, "but there is to be a death in your family."

"I suppose that is to be expected at my age," Mrs. Jones said. "Who does not have a death in the family at some point? Is that all the fortune you have for me?"

Who are the others gathered here, Charley?

"The spirits send their messages of love through me as their instrument by the law of vibrations," Lydia explained. "Like a wireless. At times the messages are unclear."

They are as clear as the sun in the sky, Charley said.

This is no time for sarcasm, Charley. Lydia's frustration mounted. She'd done readings for hundreds of people. Most went away happy, but of late, there had been more than the normal number of errors.

Her husband will die in four years, Charley said. *Tell her that. She should not marry again because she will not be content.*

Lydia sighed and repeated the message.

"My husband is over sixty years of age," Mrs. Jones said. "It does not take a fortune-teller to tell me he is getting close to meeting his maker. This is a waste of my time and money."

"I am sorry," Lydia said. This was getting embarrassing to say the least. She was not incapable of making errors, but something was amiss. "Charley is not cooperating with me at this time."

"Then maybe you shouldn't be advertising in the paper," Mrs. Jones said.

Elizabeth's mother is here, Charley said. *Tell her that.*

"I have the mother of Elizabeth here," Lydia said.

"Elizabeth?" Mrs. Jones face went pale.

Lydia could see the spirit clearly now. She was middle aged with a gray dress and white bonnet. She had her locket in the palm of her hand. Her voice was musical like a harp.

Lydia described the woman. "She says Elizabeth has her locket, the one with the curl of blond hair inside."

Mrs. Jones nodded her head almost imperceptibly.

"That is correct, is it not?" Lydia asked.

"No! I know nothing about a locket," Mrs. Jones said.

Liar, Charley said.

"Elizabeth's mother says she is sorry she left her alone in the physical world," Lydia said. "She sends her much love and affection. And she thanks you for caring for her."

"I don't ... I ..." Mrs. Jones said.

"She is happy to see you are such a God-fearing woman working for the good of your fellow brethren."

"I must be going," Mrs. Jones said.

She doesn't want to hear the truth, Charley said. *Ask her the real reason she came here.*

Mrs. Jones rummaged through her purse and tossed two quarters on the table.

"This is the work of the devil," she mumbled. She pushed back the chair and rushed down the stairs. By the time Lydia reached the landing, Mrs. Jones fled from the house with hat and coat in her arms.

"Such a strange woman," Lydia said.

She is not the first or last, Charley quipped.

CHAPTER 3

JUNE 1907: UNANNOUNCED STORMS

Lydia wiped sweat from her forehead and dragged a twisted branch across the backyard to the carriage house. What a mess. A summer storm had brought hail the size of walnuts the previous night. Leaves, stripped from the neighborhood trees, littered the grass. Her beans and peppers were buried in debris.

"You should be leaving that for Mr. Edward," Mrs. Riley called out from her back porch. Being as wide as she was tall, she leaned against the back porch railing with a groan. It creaked against her weight. "Come have a glass of iced tea. I just made some fresh this morning."

"Maybe later," Lydia said. "I am afraid my yard needs attention." Several people up the street had broken windows. Fortunately, she and Edward had not suffered much from the storm. The slate roof of their brick house looked to be intact. Their landlord, Mr. Hughes, would be happy that there was no damage to his home.

"A yard always needs attention," Mrs. Riley said. "Nothing's surer than that."

Mrs. Riley's house had not been as lucky. A large maple had fallen in the back, taking a corner of her roof with it.

"I have cookies." Mrs. Riley chuckled. "Mr. Riley always liked his macaroons. I still make them for him, God rest his soul. It's a good thing, at my age, I don't have to worry about my girlish figure."

Lydia scanned the backyard. She had hoped to get the task

finished before the heat of the day, but at the rate she was working, it would take a couple more hours to get everything moved into a single pile. A nice cold tea wouldn't take much of her time. And the macaroons did sound tempting. She rested her rake against the house and lifted her skirts to maneuver through the branches littering the side yard.

"I suppose it won't hurt to take a break," she said.

By the time Lydia reached the front porch steps, Mrs. Riley had a small table set with sweaty glasses brimming with ice chunks. Lydia removed her work gloves and sagged into a straight-backed wood chair. The cool shade was a welcome relief. If not for the constant rumble of the Sophia Furnace, it would be an ideal spot for entertaining. She imagined Mrs. Riley as a younger woman, before her hair had gone gray and her face wrinkled, welcoming women to an afternoon tea or card party.

Mrs. Riley rushed from the house with a pitcher of tea and plate of macaroons. She poured the tea. Ice cracked in the glass.

"You have to promise you'll eat at least three of these," she said as she rested the plate between the glasses. "And take some home for your mister."

The cookies did look delicious. "I promise." Lydia laughed.

"And promise me, no more storms like this last one." Mrs. Riley poured the tea and plopped into the chair across from her. "You do have special connections with the higher ups, do you not?"

"I'm afraid things don't work that way," Lydia said. "I assumed when we moved here, we would be out of tornado country. When we lived in Ohio for a time, tornadoes were common in the spring. I've seen a house that was lifted clean off its foundation and deposited right in the middle of the road."

"Oh my." Mrs. Riley pushed the plate toward Lydia. "I suppose the local spirits have no reason to bring us bad weather. But what about kidnapped spirits? Do you think the storm was caused by the curse?"

"What curse?" Lydia bit into a cookie. Coconut bloomed in her mouth.

"I thought everyone had heard," she said. "The Baumans

brought a mummy head back from Egypt. It wasn't more than two months ago. And it's right down the street, not more than a block from here."

Lydia was usually privy to most of the local gossip, but she hadn't heard about this story. "The Baumans who own the ice cream company?"

"Yes." Mrs. Riley leaned closer. "Mr. Bauman insisted they display it right there in the parlor. It has stones in the eye holes that stare at you when you come in the room."

Lydia sipped her tea.

"Mr. Bauman said they explored the tombs of the Libyan Hills and came across the tomb of some queen, Hapshet … something. Mr. Bauman calls her Sarah now. He said he removed the head, even though the locals warned him not to."

"He just took it? It sounds like Jane Austin's book."

"Exactly. *After Three Thousand Years*," Mrs. Riley said. "I have it in my library. The mummy takes revenge upon her desecrator."

"But that is just fiction."

"Fiction or not, Mr. Bauman wrapped the head in a tablecloth in Smyrna and put it in their luggage," Mrs. Riley continued. "They even showed the head to the other passengers on the ship on the way back. Apparently, customs never checked their bags when they arrived, and they brought it all the way here to New Castle."

"And who said it was cursed?" Lydia said.

"Everyone," Mrs. Riley said. "Mrs. Bauman would like to get rid of the thing, but her mister won't hear it. It gives him something to brag about."

"I don't think she has anything to worry about," Lydia said.

Mrs. Riley practically inhaled a cookie. "You haven't had any Egyptian spirits knocking on your door?"

"No," Lydia said. If there was a disquieted spirit in the neighborhood, Charley would certainly have brought it to Lydia's attention.

Alternating cookies with gossip, Mrs. Riley managed to eat more than her share of the delectable snacks. "More tea?" she asked.

"No, thank you," Lydia said. "I need to get back to work."

* * *

Lydia leaned the rake against the house and climbed two wooden steps. The screen door screeched open as she entered. She'd meant to remind Edward that the hinges needed oiled, but that always slipped her mind. The living are too busy, Charley was fond of reminding her. They are so noisy it is no wonder they cannot see or hear beyond themselves.

Lydia retrieved a large mixing bowl from under the counter. She'd put off baking in effort to get the yard work done. Now it was too hot in the kitchen, but she still needed to get the bread made. She checked the flour canister. There would be enough for four loaves of bread. All she needed was butter and yeast.

Knock. Knock.

A gentleman peered through the screen in the back door. "Crystal Mineral Springs," he said. He lifted two green bottles high enough for her to see.

"You're not the usual man," Lydia said.

"John is ill," he said. "I'm taking his route today."

"I see." Lydia moved to the back door. John was a thin man with straggly blond hair and a lazy left eye. This man was too clean-cut, too well fed with his chubby, boyish cheeks. His dark hair was parted neatly on the left and held in place with Macassar oil. He definitely wasn't the type to be delivering water.

"Quite a storm last night," he said.

"Yes." A strange feeling passed over her. She stood with the door closed. Charley? She didn't think so. If he had crossed through, it was only for a moment. There was no scent of almond.

"Some of the roads are completely blocked up on the North Hill." He shifted the bottles in his arms. "Not only do I have to deliver for two, I can't even reach some of my customers."

Lydia touched the door latch and paused. Let him in, she told herself. This was silly.

"I'm sure people will understand why the deliveries are late," she said.

"Well," he said. "You know how some of those people are up on the hill."

Lydia nodded.

"Holier than God's own angels." His boyish face broke into a grin.

Lydia opened the door and motioned for him to come inside.

"You can set them there on the table," she said.

The bottles clanked against the polished wood. The man reached into his back pocket and pulled out a folded paper.

"I've already paid for this month," Lydia said.

"Mrs. Edward H. Marquette?"

"Yes."

"You are under arrest."

He held the paper toward her. A second man strode through the back door, letting it slam behind him.

"What?" Lydia's head buzzed.

"I have a warrant for your arrest under the charge of fortune-telling."

"This must be a mistake," Lydia said.

"No, ma'am, it's no mistake."

CHAPTER 4

SUMMER 1959: SHE SEES DEAD PEOPLE

The day wasn't hot yet, but Karen knew it would be. Cicadas buzzed in the trees. They were loud enough that she heard them with her bedroom windows closed. Buzz. Buzz. They were like the Wee People, spirits, or whatever they were. Always humming in the background.

Mom rattled dishes downstairs in the kitchen. The radio played low, but Karen recognized the words to the song, "Put Your Head on My Shoulder" by Paul Anka. She didn't know all the words, but she sang along anyway.

"Not you," she said to the empty room. "No touching." Karen plopped on her bed. The Wee People didn't show themselves, but she knew they were there. She could almost feel them standing next to her or see them floating near the ceiling like white shadows. The last thing she wanted to do was invite one of them to touch her shoulder.

She scooted along the length of the bed until her back was against the front window. She squinted her eyes, trying to focus. All she could see was her dresser and cluttered closet, but she knew at least one of them was there.

Karen wondered if Mom and Dad would let her have a radio in her room. One of those little red ones she'd seen at Troutman's Department Store. Then she could keep from hearing the Wee People's buzzing. It's not that they were scary like barking dogs or thunder. As a matter of fact, she felt they were there to watch over her. Still, she didn't like having them around all the time.

"Sha bop a doodly bop," she sang. "Sha bop. Doo Doo Doo Sha bop sha bop."

When she tried to tell Mom about the Wee People, Mom would just nod. She didn't want to hear about such things. She'd made that perfectly clear to Karen. Then she blamed Grandma Obie for Karen's wild imagination. "Tell your mother to quit filling Karen's head with such nonsense," she'd told Dad. "Wee People! How can a good Catholic believe in such things?" Dad promised to talk to Obie, but Karen didn't think he ever did. Obie was stubborn. Once her mind was made up, there was no changing it. Maybe Obie figured if she went to mass every morning, it was okay to believe in other things. Maybe the Wee People were like the saints: Saint Peter, Saint Andrew, Saint Joseph. Just smaller. Wee Saints.

Karen shivered despite the room's warmth. Time to go outside. The Wee Saints, or whatever they were, wouldn't follow her out there, and she could be alone for a while. She counted the steps from her room, past the bathroom, to the top of the stairs. They didn't like it when she counted, because she couldn't hear them. One. Two. Three. There were five steps to the landing and ten more to the living room. It was a quick dash to the front door. The screen door banged open.

"Don't go out of the yard," Mom called from the kitchen.

"I won't!"

The porch overlooked their narrow front yard and gravel street. The grass was neatly trimmed, just the way Dad wanted it. Karen loved the smell of newly cut grass, but it wouldn't be cut again until Saturday when Dad was off from work.

The neighbors had parked their new car in the driveway across the road. It was blue on the bottom and white on the top. It wasn't like other cars on their street. They were boring colors, green and black, and round. Round fronts, round bumpers, round trunks. This new car sat low to the road and was squarish, angled. She liked it. When she grew up, she wanted a car like that. And a radio.

The afternoon sun suddenly glowed brightly. It bleached out the grass, the blue car, and even the sky. The noisy cicadas faded away in the radiance. Karen blinked her eyes. The air seemed thicker than normal. She smelled something. A barn. Straw.

She didn't see the man on the white horse coming up the street. He paused at the intersection near the house dressed in black with a large cowboy hat and gray bandanna tied around his neck. His saddle was polished, and he had little spurs on the back of his boots. Hopalong Cassidy, she thought.

Clip clop. Clip clop. The horse snorted as they approached. The man was tall and thin and sat straight in the saddle. At first, he didn't see her on the front steps. She thought about saying hello to him, but he was a stranger and Mom had warned her about talking to people she didn't know.

When he spotted her, he smiled and tipped his hat. She held her breath, wanting to say something.

"Howdy," he said. "It's a beautiful day." He seemed like a nice man. His voice was calming, and his eyes were gentle. "How are you?"

"I'm fine," Karen said. She wanted to ask him why he was on their street. Where was he going? Did he live around here? Cars she was used to, but she'd never seen a horse in their city neighborhood before.

The man clicked his tongue and the horse continued down the street. She watched them until they reached a large evergreen at the next corner. She couldn't tell if they turned at the intersection or continued straight ahead, but they were suddenly out of sight. A slight breeze brushed her cheek and the sun wasn't so bright.

Hairs rose on her arms and the back of her neck. He is just a regular man, Karen told herself, but she knew that wasn't the truth. Was he one of the Wee People? He must have been. Karen had always imagined them as small. This man was as large as her father. She'd have to ask Obie how big the Wee People were.

Karen ran into the house, through the living room, and back to the kitchen. Mom was busy washing dishes at the sink. Karen slid onto the alcove bench that lined the wall around the kitchen table.

"Do you want something to drink?" Mom asked. "I've got Kool-Aid."

"There was a man on a horse," Karen said. "He was riding down the street."

"A horse?" Mom looked up from the sink. "Are you sure?"

"It was a white horse," she said. "He looked like Hopalong Cassidy."

"What in the world would a man on a horse be doing here?" Mom dried her hands on a towel and left the kitchen. The screen door opened with a squeal. When she returned, she had a frown on her face. "I didn't see anyone."

"He's already gone," Karen said.

"Did he say anything to you?"

"He said hello."

"That's all?"

Karen nodded.

"I don't want you talking to men on horses," Mom said. She opened the refrigerator door. "The next time you see him, come and get me. I made cherry Kool-Aid. Do you want a cookie with it?"

Karen nodded. She would pretend to forget about the man, but she wouldn't. She'd ask Obie after church tomorrow.

* * *

"In nomine Patris, et Filii, et Spiritius Sancti," the priest called out.

"Amen," the congregation answered.

"Ominus vobiscum. Et cum spiritu tuo," he sang.

Grandma Obie sat in a middle pew. Her short hair curled around her face and her thin lips were pink with lipstick. As usual, she wore her church dress with the short sleeves and white collar.

Obie always went to early mass at St. Mary's Church. When Karen visited, she would go with her. "It's my duty as your godmother," Obie would say. "To make sure you are raised a good Catholic." Karen wasn't sure what that meant, but she liked to watch the altar boys light the candles with their long golden poles. Sometimes Obie would let her put change in a little metal box and help her light a prayer candle at the side of the church.

21

That day she prayed for the man on the horse.

Mass was said in words Karen didn't understand. Latin, Obie had told her. It was special language. Karen wondered if it was the language the saints used. Maybe the Wee People spoke Latin too.

Stand. Sit. Kneel. Everyone seemed to know what to do and when. She figured when she became a good Catholic, she would know all the words and actions.

The priest took a golden cup from a little golden box behind the altar. Karen wondered what else was hidden in the special little place. Was God in there? The priest held the cup out and said something quietly. He stood behind the altar, extended, and then joined his hands. "Orate, fratres, ut meum ac vestrum safrificium acceptabile fiat apud Deum Patrem omnipotentem."

Everyone stood. Obie read from her book. "Suscipiat Dominus sacrificium de minibus tuis ad laudem at gloriam nominis sui ad utilitatem quoque nostrum totiusque Ecclesiae suae sanctae."

The priest stood and prayed over the cup and the little wafers. Someday, Karen would be able to have a wafer, but she wasn't old enough yet. She would have to go to church school and learn all the special prayers before then.

"Amen," everyone said.

"Amen," Karen said.

Uncle John, who was living with Obie, picked them up in his car after mass. Karen crawled across the warm vinyl to sit in the middle. Obie slammed the door. It only took a couple of minutes to drive up the street. Uncle John parked the car in front of the stone wall where it opened into a set of steps. One. Two. Three. Karen counted as they climbed. Ten.

"Everyone's coming for dinner today," Obie said. "I'll need you to be my helper."

"Okay," Karen said.

The kitchen already smelled of cinnamon and sugar from the sticky buns and chocolate cookies they had made the night before. Karen liked how the dough would rise before they could bake them. While they had waited for the dough, Obie let her measure out the sugar and flour. Obie added a little spoon full of vanilla and broke the eggs.

Obie tied an apron about her waist and pulled a big pot out of the cupboard. It banged on the top of the stove. "Fetch me some potatoes," she said.

Potatoes meant potato salad. Karen couldn't wait. She ran to the cellar and loaded a basket with as many potatoes as she could carry. When she returned to the kitchen, Obie had a meat loaf tucked into a pan and was sliding it into the oven. A cabbage sat on the counter, ready to be grated into cole slaw.

"Thank you, dear." Obie lifted the basket to the sink.

Karen watched water run over the potatoes. "Do Wee People ride horses?" she asked.

"Horses?" Obie laughed. "What makes you ask that?"

"I saw a man on a horse," she said. "In front of our house."

Obie turned off the water. "Not a Wee Person," she said. "Probably a passing spirit. Did he speak to you?"

"He said hello."

Obie cut the skin off the first potato. "Next time ask him what his name is."

The front screen door slammed.

"Hello," Dad called from the living room. "We're here."

"In the kitchen," Obie said.

Mom strolled into the room with a plastic bowl. She opened the refrigerator door and rearranged containers to make room for it. Dad followed, waving a colorful Boy's Town pamphlet. "You're not sending money to these people again, are you?"

Obie glanced up from the sink. "It's none of your business."

"It's my business when you send your money to them instead of paying your bills."

"Why don't you help John set up the table and chairs," Obie said.

Before they finished peeling potatoes, Uncle Art and Aunt Chick arrived with little Art. He was older than Karen and was never interested in playing. Then came Uncle Carl and their four kids, and Uncle Ralph and Aunt Helen. They had older children too. Everyone brought something to add to the potluck, and soon the kitchen was too crowded to stand in.

Karen wandered to the backyard. Dad and Uncle John already had the tables arranged lengthwise and were putting chairs around the edge. Aunt Chick had an armload of plates and Cousin Mary Ann carried the silverware. The boys were playing catch with a baseball. Karen didn't like catch. She was afraid of being hit.

Uncle Ralph and Aunt Helen arrived with Tommy Jo and Susan. They were older too, and Karen felt alone in the group until Cousin Martin rushed from the house, golden curls bouncing. He was the only one who was her age, but he lived in Erie, so she didn't get to see him very often.

He made a beeline to Karen. "Do you wanta play?"

"Yeah," she said.

"Let's play hide-and-seek," Martin said.

"That's good," she said. It didn't matter what the game was.

The older boys were positioned across the backyard to play catch, so Karen and Martin moved back into the trees. "There's no good place to hide here," Martin said. "Let's go into the graveyard."

"Okay," Karen said. Obie didn't mind them going beyond the black iron fence, but they weren't to take anything from the graves. They learned their lesson the day they took all the little American flags from the soldiers and Obie made them put every single one back. She was really mad.

The black metal gate at the back of the yard unlatched easily and swung inward. It was only four steps from the gate to one of the gravel drives that circled around the cemetery. Ahead, two leafy maples draped over the path, making a high arch. Martin ran to a big gray stone higher than he was tall. B-O-O-K was engraved on the side. "That says book," Martin had told her. She was confused at first. It was a stone, not a book. Later, she understood that it was a person's name, like Oberleitner. There were dead people buried here. Not the people. The bodies.

"You can be *it* first," Martin said, pointing. "I'll go hide." He jumped from the stone and ran.

Karen covered her eyes and counted. "Ten," she yelled. "Here I come."

Karen wandered across the grass and back to a grove of pine

trees. The ground was covered with needles. Karen loved the smell here. It reminded her of Christmas. She didn't see Martin anywhere, but she found a tall stick to walk with.

She left the grove and stopped next to a building made of large stone blocks. Two pillars stood on each side of a metal door. A wrought-iron gate with a flower medallion stood closed in front of the door. Karen imagined it as a miniature house inside, just her size. Martin had told her they weren't allowed inside. There were coffins in there.

Karen scanned the graveyard. There were tall, pointed stones and short square ones. She liked the stones with scrolling decorations and curved tops. This place was calm and quiet, just the opposite of Obie's house where people were loud and boisterous. There weren't any Wee People here.

"Here I come," Karen said. Ahead, it looked like the graveyard ended, but there was a steep hill that led down to a group of houses and a side road where the main entrance was. Martin usually hid down there. Karen ran between the stones. Some were so small, she had to watch to keep from tripping over them.

She spotted Martin crouching behind a square gray stone, peering over the top. Dark smoke from the mill below floated into the already cloudy sky. The air was warm, but Karen's skin felt cool. Someone was here. Just for a moment. Probably passing by.

"I see you," Karen said. Martin ducked and tried to sneak to the next stone. Karen flew down the hill and nabbed him from behind. "You're it," she said.

"Okay," Martin said. He covered his eyes and counted really fast. "Ten!"

"No fair," Karen said. "I didn't have time to hide. Count again."

Martin frowned, but began to count, slower this time.

Karen followed the path to the left and charged down the hill. At the bottom, she discovered she'd left her stick. She rushed between the stones until she reached the angel and sat on the ground next to the base that was shaped like a long box. The angel was mounted at the head of the box and surrounded by a glass box. He had curly hair like Martin's, but he wore a robe that looped round one shoulder, and no shoes. One leg was perched on a rock so he could support a book on his knee. He was busy writing something in the book with a feather pen.

Karen couldn't see the book's page and wondered what he was writing. Maybe it was a story like the ones Obie told her. Maybe it was in Latin.

"I see you," Martin called. He ran toward her and tagged her shoulder. "That wasn't a very good hiding place. You're it."

"Okay. You go hide." Karen stood and hid her eyes against the glass enclosure. "One. Two. Three." She imagined that if she broke the glass, the angel would come alive. "Four. Five. Six." It would be free to fly into the sky. Up to heaven. "Seven. Eight. Nine." Maybe it would leave its book behind and she would see its message. "Ten! Here I come."

CHAPTER 5

MAY 1907: A COMING TRIAL

The aroma of roasting chicken filled the kitchen, overtaking the more unpleasant street smells of sewage and horse manure that filtered into the house in summer. Lydia used the edge of her apron to lift the lid of the potato pot. She wasn't sure she'd ever get used to this new gas stove. It heated everything much more quickly than the old coal burner.

The back door banged shut. Lydia's heart raced. She expected to see Detective Logan rushing into the kitchen with one of his henchmen. Instead, it was Edward.

"Lottie, you'll ..." Edward's hair was askew, as if he'd been running. A curl of dark hair hung down across his forehead.

"What's wrong?" She replaced the pot lid and picked up a fork from the counter. Were the police coming?

"Nothing's wrong," Edward said. He set his lunch pail on the kitchen table.

"Don't startle me like that," she said.

"Sorry." He loosened his tie and took off his dispatching jacket. "I was excited. We got to see the president."

Lydia sighed and looked at the floor. Edward's shoes were caked with dried mud.

"I just scrubbed this floor yesterday," she said.

"Sorry," he said. "I forgot." He untied his shoes and kicked them off near the door mat.

"You might be a new dispatcher meeting all sorts of railroad big wigs," she said. "But I'll not have you tracking up my house."

"I didn't see the railroad president." He laughed. "I saw *The President*. Teddy Roosevelt."

"You're joking."

"He came through on the train," Edward said. "It stopped at Ellwood City and then at New Castle junction. There was a big crowd of railroaders. They let us leave our desks to see him. I didn't believe it until he stepped right out on the rear platform. He waved and started shaking hands."

"You don't say."

"I wasn't close enough for a handshake, but I did get to see him. He looks just like he does in the newspaper."

"The President of the United States," she said. "Right here in New Castle. Who would have thought it possible?"

"Madigan said he's probably on his way out west, to shoot some game."

Lydia turned the fire off under the potatoes. "It would be nice to go back." She hadn't seen Colorado since she'd moved away. That was at least ten years.

"No, thank you," Edward said. "Too many earthquakes out that way for my taste."

Lydia poured water from the potatoes into the sink. Steam erupted, bathing her in warmth.

"I didn't mean San Francisco," she said. "I'd like to see Yellowstone Park."

She recalled photographs she'd seen of the geysers and forests. They even had bison there. Some scenes looked like another world. It was amazing how one country could hold so many wonders.

"When I'm president of the railroad," Edward said, "we will take the train to Yellowstone."

Lydia laughed. "Right now, I want you to take yourself out of my kitchen. Wash up for supper."

"Yes, ma'am." He smacked her on the derriere as he passed.

* * *

Lydia had just finished the last of the dishes when there was

28

a light rap on the back door. Alice Stansfield stood on the top step with her hand cupped above her brow so she could see inside. Alice was an experienced medium who was involved with the people up at the Lily Dale spiritualist center in New York. She and her husband, William, had apparently been involved with a spiritualist organization when they lived in England. Lydia wasn't sure how they'd ended up in New Castle.

Lydia dried her hands on her apron. "Come in," she said. "What brings you here this time of the evening?"

"A promise to be fulfilled," she said in a heavy British accent. She stepped inside and peered over wire-framed spectacles. "It is a bit brisk for this time of year, isn't it?"

"Yes," Lydia said. "The *Farmer's Almanac* predicts a cooler than normal summer."

"And the law threatens to put us in jail for fortune-telling." Alice walked into the kitchen and set her heavily embroidered bag on the table. She rummaged through it and removed a large tome. "This is the book I promised you," she said.

Lydia didn't remember asking for a book, but she and Alice had so many conversations about Spiritualism she couldn't be expected to remember them all.

Alice handed her the cloth-bound copy. "*The Magic Staff* by Andrew Jackson Davis."

"He was the healer?"

"He was an uneducated man from the back country. No schooling. No training," Alice said. "He was put in a mesmerizing trance one day and began to see the other side more clearly than anyone else since."

Lydia flipped through the pages. "He came before the Fox sisters?"

"About the same time," Alice said. "This is his autobiography. I think you'll find it interesting. He writes quite eloquently for a man with only a couple of weeks of formal education."

"I will begin reading tomorrow," Lydia said.

Alice put her hands on her hips. "So, how are you holding up?"

"I try not to think about it," Lydia said. "But the trial is in two weeks. I don't know what I'll do if I go to jail."

"You'll not be going to jail," Alice said.

"I can't be sure of that."

"This trial is just another stunt instigated by the Temperance Society," Alice said. "If they had their way, they'd take all our freedoms. Mark my words, plenty of people are angry with their shenanigans, including the politicians."

"My lawyer said we have a good case, but I'm not so certain."

Alice rummaged through her bag again. "Did you see what Councilman Genkinger said? It was in yesterday's paper."

"I've been trying not to read the paper."

Alice slid a folded newspaper from her bag. She opened it and adjusted her glasses.

"Listen to this," she said. "Genkinger called the Temperance Society, and I quote, 'parasites, men who are desirous of getting up their batting average and suffer brainstorms, men who cowardly sneak into the gallery at the Opera House, witness a burlesque show, and bring persecutions for the production of an immoral attraction.'"

Lydia didn't know Mr. Genkinger, but she knew the Genkingers owned the Opera House. Were the only people willing to support her saloon owners, dancers, and beer makers?

"Genkinger even mentioned you," Alice said. "The paper says, 'Mr. Genkinger even included as marks for his arraignment, the eight or more prominent women of the city who secured the evidence upon which Mrs. Marquette, the fortune-teller, was held for trial at the June term of court by Alderman Morrison. To these he referred as women who "Through deception, which is the counterpart of lying, had secured their evidence and then turned it to the use of the prosecution in the case."'"

"Let me see that," Lydia said. It was there in black and white, right on the front page. "Logan and All Law-enforcers Are Attacked by Genkinger in Bitter Speech in Councils." She hoped Alice was right, and there were enough people in the city sympathetic to her plight, that she would be exonerated. It was difficult to remain hopeful. Alice hadn't seen the looks on the women's faces during Lydia's hearing. She hadn't seen the scowling ministers in the audience. If they had their way, Lydia would go to jail for the rest of her life.

"You see," Alice said. "The spirit people are nudging others to speak up against this profanation. They won't let you be wrongly convicted."

Lydia stared at the paper. She hadn't spoken to Charley in weeks. Were Genkinger's words a sign that the spirit people were supporting her? She felt as if she had abandoned them.

"I've picked up several of your clients since you closed your doors," Alice said. "Everyone asks about you. You are not alone in this."

Lydia folded the paper. "If only *they* were my jurors," she said. Her lawyer insisted that she would get a fair trial by a jury of her peers. Most of Lydia's clients were women with an interest in Spiritualism. There would be twelve men sitting in judgment. They would undoubtedly be mill workers, shopkeepers, tailors, or grocers. Most, if not all, would be members of traditional churches: Methodist, Presbyterian, Catholics. She had few peers in this city.

"Now, now," Alice said. "Don't be so glum."

"I wish it were June," Lydia said. "This infernal waiting is worse than a jail sentence."

Alice patted her on the shoulder. "Nothing like a good book to pass the hours," she said. "After you've read Mr. Davis, I have one by William Britten entitled *Nineteenth Century Miracles*. I also have a piece about the Fox sisters written in '74 by a William Crooks."

Lydia forced a smile. She usually had a positive disposition, but the passing weeks had taken their toll.

"We could always take a trip up to Lily Dale," Alice said. "It's a nice train ride."

Lydia hadn't been to the Spiritualist community in two summers. It would be a relief to get away from the city. She imagined herself sitting on the dock, dangling her feet in the cool lake water. She could attend a session at the Healing Temple and a Saturday night reading. If only for a day or two, she would be able to breathe free again.

CHAPTER 6

FALL 1966: PAJAMA PARTY

Karen kneeled on the couch with her friends, looking out the front window of the living room. All the leaves were off the trees, but they hadn't had any snow yet. Expect it any day now, her mom had said. It wasn't uncommon to get snow before Thanksgiving in Pennsylvania.

The Beatles' newest hit, "Eleanor Rigby," played on the radio. Karen didn't know all the words so she hummed along.

An old brown sedan with rusted fenders pulled up along the street in front of the house. Sandy sprang from the car, her black ponytail whipping in the breeze. She was the last one coming to the party. Karen didn't know her as well as the other girls. Barb, Linda, and Donna went to seventh grade at Ben Franklin School with her. Sandy was a year younger and attended George Washington School in Mahoningtown. She was Barb's friend.

Karen opened the door. Sandy waved at her dad and rushed inside. The cold air was laden with the odor of burning leaves. Sandy dropped her overnight bag on a chair and let her coat slip from her shoulders. "The boys are out there," she said.

"Where?" Barb said. She pulled back her blond hair and peered out the front door. "I don't see anyone."

"They're down at the corner hanging around."

Barb mashed her face up against the glass. "Who?"

"I don't know," Sandy said. "A tall guy with a red jacket and a shorter guy with glasses."

"Does the boy with the red jacket have black hair?"

"I don't remember." Sandy shivered. "I think so."

"My mom said we can go up to the third floor," Karen said. If she didn't prod them, they would be watching for boys all evening. Karen liked boys, too, but that wouldn't be any fun. "Come on, let's go up."

The girls grabbed their bags. Karen took the lead. When she was younger, she never would have invited friends over to the house. The spirit people who normally hung out on the second floor were too distracting. In the last few years, she didn't see them as much. She wasn't sure if they weren't there or if she was able to keep herself from seeing them. She'd read something about psychics being able to block the spirits out of their heads. Maybe that's what was happening.

Karen rounded the corner and took the steps to the third floor. It was best not to mention spirits. The girls would call them ghosts and think they were something to be afraid of. She wished she had special goggles like in the movie she'd seen on Chiller Theater with Chilly Billy. It was called *13 Ghosts*. In the movie, Dr. Zorba had died, leaving his mansion and hidden fortune to his nephew. With the magical goggles his uncle left him, the nephew could see the ghosts living in the house.

The third floor wasn't entirely finished, but it did have a kitchenette because people had lived up there at one time. The only windows were at each end of the long attic room. There wasn't any furniture, only some chairs, her record player and records stacked near the outlet.

Barb rushed to the window and peered out. The wooden floor squeaked under her feet. "I don't see any boys down there," she said. "Are you sure you saw them?"

"This is so cool," Sandy said. "It would be great to live up here."

"Yeah," Karen said. "I've thought about it, but Mom says it's too hot in the summer."

Linda and Donna made a beeline to the records and sat cross-legged on the floor. "What do you want to hear?" Linda asked.

"The Beatles are my favorite," Karen said.

"We Can Work It Out" echoed through the room. "Last Train

to Clarksville" was next. Everyone danced like they were on *American Bandstand*. Karen took breaks to change the records. She thought they danced as well as everyone on TV.

"What's in here?" Barb asked, pointing to one of the small doors leading to the attic space along the sides of the room.

Karen shrugged. "Just stuff." She'd gotten locked into the attic cubby one day when she'd been snooping through things. She hadn't realized the doors could only be opened from the outside until one closed behind her and she couldn't get out. It was summer and the narrow space was like an oven. Thank goodness, Mom heard her yelling for help.

"You'll never guess what I found." Barb crawled from the cubbyhole with a flat box. "A Ouija board!" She dusted off the top.

"Put that back," Linda said. "We don't want no evil spirits coming after us."

"What's the matter?" Barb said. "Are you afraid?"

"Yes. And you should be too."

"Booooo," Donna said.

Barb opened the box. The plastic heart-shaped planchette fell to the floor and skidded along the wood.

"I mean it," Linda said. "You can bring the devil right up from the underworld with one of those things. An evil spirit can attach itself to you and follow you home."

"It doesn't work that way," Karen said.

"How do you know?" Linda narrowed her eyes.

Karen didn't want them thinking she was strange. "The Ouija board was used by Spiritualists to talk to the dead," she blurted out. "I read about it in a book."

Or maybe Obie had told her about it before she died. Karen wished Obie was still alive today. She knew things that she never told Karen, more than just about Wee People. When Mom and Dad moved Obie into a new apartment on Halco Drive, Obie wasn't happy. It was a nice apartment, but she kept running away to live with friends on Neshannock Avenue down by the river. Dad complained about those "strange" people down there. Karen had never met any of them, but she wondered if they talked to spirits like Obie.

She almost asked Dad about the people on Neshannock Avenue but knew he would shrug it off. Obie was old and maybe a little dementia had set in by then. It wasn't until she ended up in the nursing home toward the end that she stopped running off. Now it was too late to ask her.

"It's just a game," Barb said. "Look. It's made by Parker Brothers."

"It was also made in Salem, Massachusetts," Linda said. "As in *Salem Witch Trials*."

"I'm not afraid of it," Sandy said. "Who wants to do it with me?"

"I will," Karen said. She'd played around with it before. It might help normal people talk to the spirits, but to her it was like trying to talk to someone through a wall. Why work through a barrier when you could sense the spirits directly?

They sat with the planchette centered on the board. Karen rested her fingers lightly on the plastic. Barb hovered over them, blue eyes darting back and forth.

"Hello? Is anyone there?" Sandy asked.

The planchette remained still. "Paperback Writer" played on the record player. Linda turned up the sound.

"Are you there?" Sandy asked a second time.

The planchette slid to the YES. Barb squatted beside them. "Is your house haunted?"

"No," Karen said. She wasn't lying. The spirits she knew were there to watch over her. They weren't trapped in the house. It wasn't haunted.

"Are you an evil spirit?" Sandy said.

The planchette slid to the NO.

"See," Sandy said. "There are no evil spirits here."

"I'm not listening," Linda said.

Questions and answers were a slow process. One letter after the other. Question after question. Yes. No. Karen's mind wandered. She thought she smelled chocolate cookies.

"Who am I going to marry?" Sandy asked.

The planchette slid to the L and then the N before stopping.

35

"L. N.," Sandy said. "That can't be right. Those aren't the right initials."

"L. N.," Barb said. "Who's L. N.?"

"I don't know," Sandy said. "I don't know anyone with those initials."

"It doesn't have to be someone you know now," Barb said. "Let me try."

Karen gladly gave up her spot to Barb. They asked questions for a while, but Barb was unhappy with the answers. Linda looked bored and Donna was lying on her back reading a teen magazine that she'd brought. This party was turning into a flop.

"Hey, girls," Karen's mom called from the foot of the steps. "It's almost time for *The Wizard of Oz*."

"Okay, Mom." Karen had watched the movie every year for as long as she could remember. She was a teenager now, but it was a tradition. She always thought the scariest part was when Dorothy stared into the giant hourglass and Auntie Em turned into the wicked witch.

They put on their pajamas and created a nest of blankets on the living room floor. Mom didn't fail them. They had cookies and milk to go with the movie and other snacks later.

That was the only time they used the Ouija board. As Karen grew older, she was determined to be normal. She became more interested in boys. She even dated Steve from her homeroom. He was just the opposite of her in looks, tall and blond, with blue eyes. Like her, he was a Beatles fan. He even gave her a copy of the *Rubber Soul Album*. Sandy didn't marry the boy of her junior high dreams, but when she did marry, the man's initials were L. N., just as the Ouija board had predicted.

CHAPTER 7

JUNE 1907: THE TRIAL BEGINS

Lydia breathed deeply and followed Attorney Aiken into the courtroom. The dark-paneled walls felt like they were closing in around her. The chamber erupted in whispers. She could only imagine what they were saying. Charlatan. Imposter. Devil worshiper. Witch. Some were serious about their Christian beliefs and undoubtedly hoped she would hang. Others were there for the entertainment.

Aiken pushed between folding chairs that had been added to accommodate the mass of people. The room brimmed with women dressed in their finest: lace gloves, feathered hats, and polished shoes. Men, mostly ministers that Lydia recognized from the preliminary trial, sat erect, rigid collars chaffing their throats. Attorney Young and James Chambers from the prosecution sat at a table to the right, as ironed and poised as their suits.

Lydia slowed, allowing Edward's meaty hand to press against the small of her back. She wanted his hand in hers, his arms around her. That would probably be as unseemly as fortune-telling.

"Half the city is here," he whispered. The Black Hand murder trials had been so crowded, people had been turned away. Now that those convictions were ended, this was the new show in town. Edward motioned for her to sit next to the Aikens. Lydia held her chin high and sat gingerly on the hard seat.

"It's turned into a circus," she said. She'd chosen a conservative black dress to reflect her seriousness and professionalism. No doubt, these women expected a gypsy clad in bangles and colorful skirts. "Maybe it was a mistake, agreeing not to speak on my own behalf."

"Mr. Aiken knows his business," Edward whispered in her ear. "Besides, you know you would not be able to keep from lecturing to the room on the true meaning of Spiritualism." He winked.

"I suppose you're right," she said.

No sooner had they seated themselves than a group of sober-looking jurymen entered from an adjoining chamber. They took places at the front of the room, left of the judge's bench.

Edward leaned toward her. "You worried for nothing," he said. "The jury looks positively understanding, a fine group of law-abiding citizens who 'sneak into the Opera House to witness a burlesque show.'"

Lydia held back a smile. Hopefully, he was right, and these stern-looking men would see the hypocrisy of this case.

A slightly built man in a tweed suit took his place before the crowd. "Hear ye, hear ye," he called. "The Honorable Judge Porter's court is now in session. All rise."

The crowd quieted. The swish of dresses replaced the silence as the crowd stood. Judge Porter entered. He was a middle-aged man with a round face and full lips. He looked pleasant, maybe even pleasant enough to dismiss the case, but it was the jury who would decide Lydia's fate. She scanned their faces, hoping to find some comfort. There was nothing. They could have been mannequins in a store window.

After short introductory statements, District Attorney Young called Mrs. Mary Stratton to the stand. Mrs. Stratton took her place beside Judge Porter and sat smug faced with gloved hands resting neatly on her lap. Lydia bristled at the thought she'd been so naïve as to invite Reverend Stratton's wife into her home. The old bitty had been as polite as you please. She had seemed impressed with Lydia's reading the first time and asked for a second appointment to continue.

"Mrs. Stratton, would you tell the court on what dates you visited Mrs. Marquette?"

Mrs. Stratton focused on Attorney Young. "March thirtieth

and April first," she said.

"And would you please tell the jury about your experience?"

"When I went to her home March thirtieth," Mrs. Stratton said, "we went to an upstairs room where she proceeded to gather her wits about her, or should I say spirits. If she spoke to those spirits, I could not tell. Mrs. Marquette asked me if I would be alarmed if she told me of a death in the family. I told her I would not. She never did say who was supposed to die. She then made several unsuccessful attempts to tell the number of persons in our family."

"That is not what happened," Lydia whispered to Attorney Aiken. He patted her hand.

"So, you are saying that Mrs. Marquette was inaccurate?" Attorney Young asked.

"Yes," Mrs. Stratton said. "She informed me that three years ago I had undergone an operation, and that there was an inch in my spine through which the blood did not pass. I told her that she was mistaken. I had had no such surgery."

"And when you confronted her about these errors, what did she say?"

"When she found that she was not *reading* my past correctly she seemed to grow very indignant at the spirits. She said, 'Charley, Charley, why don't you give me the truth?'" Mrs. Stratton straightened her posture. "Mrs. Marquette remarked that she was mad at the spirits. They sometimes got stubborn."

Whispers spread about the room.

"And who is Charley?"

"I wouldn't know," Mrs. Stratton said. "I never saw this Charley. He is supposed to be a spirit guide."

Chairs creaked.

"And Mrs. Marquette spoke with this man?"

"Yes," Mrs. Stratton said. "She practices necromancy."

"She speaks with the dead?"

"Yes."

The crowd erupted.

"What?" Lydia stood. "How dare you!"

"Order in the courtroom!" the crier called out.

Edward grabbed Lydia at her waist and pulled her back to her seat. "Shh," he said.

"How can she say that?" Lydia sputtered. "I'll wager she doesn't even know what the word means. Never has anyone accused me of speaking to dead bodies. I ..."

"Order."

The crowd settled down, but Lydia remained livid. Not one woman had mentioned necromancy during the preliminary trial. They must have been coached by the prosecutor to say such a mean and hateful thing. What sort of Christians were these women?

"And you went to visit Mrs. Marquette a second time?" Attorney Young continued.

"Yes," Mrs. Stratton said. "The second time I visited, she told me my husband would live about four years, but that I should not marry again as I would not be contented."

Lydia bit her lower lip. That old witch would never be contented.

The prosecution had no more questions and Attorney Aiken stood. On cross-examination, the witness stated that Mrs. Marquette had not felt her head, used cards, or consulted the stars, and that she claimed to be a medium, not a fortune-teller.

Mrs. Edith Martin, wife of Reverend J. S. Martin of the Reformed Presbyterian Church, took the stand next. She nervously fiddled with a curl that had come lose from her coiffure and avoided glancing in Lydia's direction.

"Would you tell the court on what date you went to see Mrs. Marquette?"

"I went to Mrs. Marquette on March 29," she said. "I was met at the door by Mrs. Marquette. I asked the price and she said fifty cents."

Mrs. Martin went on to repeat a story very similar to the previous testimony. She stated that Lydia failed to tell her the correct number in her family. She said that Lydia claimed she was contemplating a second marriage when she already had a husband. She explained that Lydia told her that her next husband was to be a large, broad-shouldered man. When she informed

Lydia that she was married, Lydia dropped the subject.

"She next told me that I had my carpet up and was going to move," Mrs. Martin said. "I told her that I indeed had the carpet up, for housecleaning. It was spring, after all. Every woman in the city has her carpets up."

Some of the jurymen lost their stern composure at that statement. Laughter rang through the crowd.

"She said that I would live to be sixty-three or seventy years old," Mrs. Martin continued. "If that is not fortune-telling, I don't know what is."

Attorney Aiken matched the prosecutions questions with only one of his own. "Did the defendant ever claim to be a fortune-teller?"

"Why, no," Mrs. Martin said. "I asked her if she was the woman who told fortunes, she said that she was not a fortune-teller, but that she gave readings."

"Thank you," Attorney Aiken said. "I have nothing more."

The trial continued with Mrs. Mame Rice, whom Lydia knew as Mrs. Jones, a deaconess in the Methodist Church. She testified that Mrs. Marquette had asked Charley to tell how many people were in her family. She made two bad guesses.

She said that Mrs. Marquette was angered by Charley's stupidity and cautioned Mrs. Rice to tell her the truth. She explained that she was also told that after three years she would marry a tall, broad-shouldered man and be very happy.

"That's a lie," Lydia whispered. "They are all lies."

Mrs. Smith, wife of Professor I. L. Smith, followed with her testimony. She said that Charley told Mrs. Marquette that her husband was getting baldheaded and was jealous of a broad-shouldered young man; that her husband would die and she would marry this young man and be happy. Nancy Van Gorder testified next that Mrs. Marquette made a mistake in telling many things in connection with her family.

By the time they recessed for lunch at noon, Lydia was so distraught she couldn't eat the cold ham sandwiches Edward had so kindly made. She forced herself to imbibe a cup of tea and some soda crackers. When they returned to Aiken's office,

Lydia pleaded with him to let her testify on her own behalf. "It is obvious that these women have been coached," she said. "They all tell the same story. Even if I were a fortune-teller, would I not create a unique story for each person?"

"What is obvious to you will be obvious to the jury," Attorney Aiken assured her. "Give them the benefit of the doubt. They will see the motive behind this witch hunt."

"How can you be so sure of that?"

"Have faith in Attorney Aiken," Edward said. "There are others that will speak for you."

Despite her protests, Lydia did not take the stand in her own defense that afternoon. Other witnesses came forward to confirm that Spiritualism was considered by some to be a form of religion. Reverend Vosler traveled all the way from Columbus, Ohio. Although the prosecution raised many objections to some of the more important questions about mediumship, Vosler claimed to be a Spiritualist and explained several points about the religion. Mrs. William Becker and Mrs. James Peebles of the city and several women from Sharon were also called to testify to their belief in Spiritualism.

Lydia watched the jury. She couldn't tell if the men were swayed by the testimony or not. Half of them didn't appear to be paying attention. One white-haired man looked to be falling asleep in the warm room. Lydia imagined them all falling into a stupor and sleeping like Rip Van Winkle for one hundred years. Maybe by then, Spiritualism would be accepted, and she would be free to practice as she pleased. There would be a Spiritualist church in the city, maybe more than one. They would get the respect that they deserved.

After the last of the testimony concluded, Attorney Aiken marched up to the judge and turned to the jury. "I do not believe in Spiritualism!" he shouted. The jurymen were suddenly alert. "Just as I do not believe in Buddhism, Hinduism, Judaism, or Islam."

He paced across the room and faced the audience.

"While I do not believe in Spiritualism," he said in a quieter tone, "I have more toleration for the religious views of others than some people."

He pointed to Lydia. "My client is a member of a religion that believes in mediumship. A medium is one who has the power to get into communication with spirits of the departed."

"You and I do not believe in it," he argued, "but there are people who do believe it and we have a duty to respect their opinions."

"I ask the members of the jury," he said focusing his attention on them, "was there anything in Mrs. Marquette's conduct to show that she was not sincere? She insisted that she was not a fortune-teller, but a medium. The defendant's witnesses honestly believe in Spiritualism and her ability."

Attorney Aiken looked to the heavens. "The holy ghost is a spirit," he said. "In a good old-fashioned Methodist meeting what is it that causes the worshipers to become filled with enthusiasm and shout Glory to God? What is it but spirit?"

"You could not get a Covenanter so full of the spirit from head to foot that he would shout Amen." He shook his head. "The spirit does not move him in the same way as it does the Methodist. So, I say that Spiritualism is also different and those who practice it are not moved in the same way."

"A man dies; the materialist says that ends it. Another says that the spirit has merely left the body and so we have all kinds of belief regarding the spirit until we come to the spiritualist who believes that all is spirit." Attorney Aiken looked to Lydia. She had never seen him so animated. If this didn't sway the jury, nothing would.

"Reverend Martin in his sermons tells you what becomes of the just and the unjust. Is he foretelling future events? No, not as contemplated, but the act of assembly. Why are so many ministers here this afternoon? It is because the trial involves the question of religion."

There were whispers and a shaking of heads by ministers at this statement. They had been caught in their own trap.

Attorney Aiken countered claims that the future had been foretold by cards, tokens, symbols, and by consulting the stars when nothing of the kind was shown in the testimony. In the end, he pointed to the prosecution.

"If Reverend Martin and the state chose to punish my client for her religious beliefs," he said, "will they find your beliefs unacceptable next?"

Aiken ended with the question hanging in the air. If the jurymen were impressed by the speech, Lydia couldn't tell. Not one looked her way.

Attorney James Chambers stood promptly. "We do not deny the right of people to their religious beliefs, neither do we deny the right of individuals to practice their beliefs, so long as they do not transgress our laws. There was one sect that worshiped the sun. It was their belief that the sun was God. He would have the right to his belief. He could even offer up a sacrifice of the most beautiful woman to be found, but the laws of Pennsylvania would step in and say Thou shalt not commit murder.

"This case is not a question of religious belief. It is a question of whether Mrs. Marquette professed to foretell the future for money. If she did, she is guilty under the act."

Attorney Chambers restated the testimony as if he assumed the jurymen were thick in the head. He tried to write off the defense testimony as information but having nothing to do with the case. The question to be solved was whether or not Mrs. Marquette had professed to tell the future for money.

"I am not a fortune-teller," Lydia whispered to Edward. "That should be blatantly obvious."

Edward took her hand. "By tomorrow, you will be proclaimed innocent," he said.

She prayed he was right.

CHAPTER 8

JUNE 1907: JURY DECISION

Lydia sat between Edward and Mr. Aiken donning her most confident expression. The courtroom was even more packed than the day before if that was possible. It was probably because her trial had made the front page. It was embarrassing to be sure, but maybe her case would do Spiritualism more good than harm.

The jurymen entered and took their seats. Some conversed as if they were seated at a ball game. Was that a good sign or bad? Wouldn't they be more serious if they were about to convict her? Or maybe they were happy she was going to jail.

"All stand," the court crier announced. "The Honorable Judge Porter."

Lydia took a deep breath and stood. It would all be over soon. She could move ahead in her life, be it at home or in prison. Judge Porter sat and the crowd followed suit.

"Are your prepared?" Edward clasped Lydia's gloved hand. He'd even worn gloves that day, for protection. Word was out that another case of smallpox had been confirmed in the city. That's what should have been on the front page, not this trial.

"Has the jury made a decision?" the judge asked.

A man with a neatly trimmed beard stood. "Yes, Your Honor." He passed a paper to the crier.

Lydia imagined herself in a prison cell. They could take her away from her physical home, but not her spiritual one. She would still have Charley. But what of Edward? No one would be there in the evening to greet him, to massage his sore shoulders, to make sure he ate a decent meal. In the book Alice had lent her, Andrew Jackson Davis said, "Everything is designed to subserve an end, a purpose, in the vast and boundless laboratory of the All-wise Divine Mind." Lydia hoped that was true.

"And what is your decision?" Judge Porter asked.

"We find the defendant not guilty of the charge of fortune-telling," the man said. "Under unanimous decision."

The court erupted. Some applauded. Others hissed. One woman stood and stomped from the room.

Not Guilty. At first the words didn't register with Lydia. She was sure these men would convict her.

"This is a travesty!" Mrs. Stratton said from behind her.

Unanimous. They had *all* proclaimed her innocence. Take that, all you pretentious old biddies. Lydia turned in her chair. "So much for your witch hunt."

"God will see to it that you burn in the fires of hell," Mrs. Stratton said.

"Order in the court," the crier called.

"Lydia." Edward clasped her shoulder and forced her to face forward. "Now is not the time for arguments."

Lydia glanced from Judge Porter to the jury. A younger man in the back row with round spectacles nodded once and looked away. The jury had seen through their lies.

With the decision made, there was nothing to hold the gawkers. The crowd filtered from the room as the lawyers went on to discuss the costs of the case. A majority of the jury was for placing the costs on Reverend Martin since he had initiated the court proceedings. One elderly man held out against this. Finally, a compromise was reached, and the jury divided the costs which amounted to about $100, between the prosecutor and the defendant. Fifty dollars was a lot of money, but Lydia was too happy with the verdict to be upset with the decision. They would cut household expenses to pay for the fee.

By the time all the issues were dealt with and Lydia was dismissed, the courtroom was nearly empty. She rose from her seat and exited behind Attorney Aiken without glancing at the Reverend Martin and his wife. Outside the courthouse, thick smoke from the Sophia Furnace curled across the treetops in the warm breeze, bringing with it a foul metallic odor. Lydia's chest tightened.

Attorney Aiken rattled on about fees and legal matters. Edward nodded, but didn't appear to be listening. Lydia pulled a kerchief from her sleeve and put it over her mouth. Her throat squeezed. Not now, she thought.

"My secretary will prepare the papers for you to sign," Aiken said.

"Edwar ..." Lydia put a hand to her throat and bent forward. She gasped for air.

Edward took her by the elbow. "The asthma again?"

Lydia nodded.

"Don't worry," he said.

Attorney Aiken frowned. "Is she in need of a doctor?"

"No," Edward said. He wrapped his arm about her waist. "This happens sometimes. I just need to get her home."

"I have a ..."

A buggy pulled up to the base of the courthouse's steps. "This way," Alice Stansfield called from the passenger side. "We will give you a ride."

Their brown mare snorted and pawed the ground. Mr. Stansfield tipped his hat and motioned them forward.

"You'd best take care of your wife's health," Aiken said. "I will contact you later about the fees."

"Thank you," Edward said. "We appreciate all you have done for us."

It was kind of the Stansfields to help, but Lydia didn't want to impose. Her chest was so tight that she couldn't get out the words. Edward helped her down the steps and into the back of the buggy.

"Oh my," Alice said. "This is a bit of a row, isn't it? Let's get you to our house. I have just the thing for those lungs of yours."

Lydia's chest was on fire. Her ears rang as she tried to suck in air. Air. Any air. Even this dirty city air was preferable to nothing.

Edward rubbed her back. "Relax," he said. "You've been through this before. Give it some time. It will resolve."

Mr. Stansfield called out to the horse, encouraging it to move faster up the grade on Mill Street, but its hoofs continued to clomp along the brick at a slow, steady pace. When they finally reached Moody Avenue, it slowed even further to take a right turn.

Lydia fought for puffs of air. *It can't be my time.* Charley would be there with her, waiting to help her pass over to the other side. Wouldn't he? Her face flushed with heat. This is what it would be like to drown, heart pounding faster and faster for fresh air that was never to come.

"Almost home," Alice said. "Almost home."

When they reached the new four-square house, Lydia was too light-headed to walk. Edward, dear Edward, scooped her into his arms and carried her up the front steps. What would she have done without his support and approval all these years? If it hadn't been for him, she would never have developed her medium skills.

The house was a symphony of flowers: wallpaper of light pink roses, green brocade curtains with a lily design, vases of mixed flowers and a painting of an English garden. The green sofa was the only print-free surface.

"On the sofa," Alice said. "Lilly! We need some help here."

Edward lowered her gently and knelt beside her. His brow furrowed with worry. I'm sorry, she thought. She hated to put him through this. He should have a healthy partner, not one who fought to stay alive at times like these.

"What is it, Momma?" Lilly entered the room. She was thin and fine boned with mousy brown hair.

"Get the cold balm from upstairs, will you?"

Wood creaked on the main stairs. Lydia forced her lungs to move, but it was as if a train engine had parked on top of her. She closed her eyes. Maybe it would be better to let go of this life and all the suffering. Charley? Are you here?

"Is this it?" Lilly asked.

"Yes," Alice said, unscrewing the cap. "Let's give this a try."

The pungent aromas of camphor and mustard oil burned Lydia's nose. Her eyes watered. Hands worked to sit her upright, unbuttoning and removing her blouse. The salve Alice applied to her chest was cold, then hot.

"Rest easy," Alice said. "Let the medicine do its work."

Lydia laid back. In. Out. Her lungs rattled like old bellows.

"I'll make some garlic milk," Alice said. She stood with a groan. "That is sure to do the trick."

Pots clanked in the kitchen. William Stansfield trotted into the room from back of the house. Forgetting to remove his hat and coat, he paced the length of the room, wringing his hands.

"She'll be fine," Edward said.

William nodded, but still looked concerned.

Edward squeezed her hand. "She has these spells from time to time."

"There's no excuse for it," William muttered. "We have found ourselves in a city of bitter and malicious clergy. There was no reason that this good woman should have been subjected to such a vicious undertaking. You would think we were still living during the Inquisition. Is this not the twentieth century?"

Lilly peered from the kitchen, looking concerned. Lydia's breathing eased but she dared not speak.

"New Castle has had its own witch trial," William continued. "Did they think they could prove she was deceptive with their lies? And these are supposed men and women of the church. The public have the right to ask questions of these religious leaders. We are living in what is called a free country. No person should be dubbed heretic, unbeliever, secularist, atheist, or any other name because they demand answers to questions of great import."

Alice entered the room with a tray holding a glass of milk and a jar with a gold-colored concoction. She placed the tray on a side table and wiped her hands on her apron. "That is enough of your soapbox, William. Let's let the poor woman recover, before you send her into another spasm."

"Sorry," William said.

"Take off your hat and coat," Alice said. She mixed the gold sauce into the steaming milk and handed it to Lydia. "Breathe this 'til it cools."

"It's this damned city air," William said. "Not fit for man nor beast."

The milk stank of garlic, but the grip on Lydia's lungs eased. She breathed deeply.

"It's passing," Edward said. "Thank God. You always worry me at times like these."

"As soon as it cools, I want you to drink it all down," Alice said.

Lydia grimaced. She'd had enough concoctions for one day. "This is ginger, pomegranate, honey, and fenugreek seed." This mixture smelled appetizing at least. Lydia opened wide and swallowed it quickly.

"She's pinking up nicely," Alice said.

Lydia inched up. "I am feeling better," she said. "Thank you for all your help. I didn't mean to put you out."

"It's nothing," Alice said. "We need to stand together."

"It's time we do more than stand," William said. "This city needs to crawl out of the dark ages. I am writing to the editor. Things need to be said."

Lydia nodded. They could start with letters, but would it do any good? What they needed was respect and recognition.

"We need to start a church," Alice said.

CHAPTER 9

SUMMER 1968: RIDE BOYS AND GYPSIES

Karen helped Dad unload boxes from the trunk at the Lawrence County Farm Show. It was only ten in the morning and already the August sun was hot. Dust hung in the air. Two years ago, the fair had moved to this new, larger location along Harlansburg Road. There was more grass here, but in a few hours all the tents would be up, the rides and food trucks would be parked, and it would all be trampled.

Since Mom worked full-time, Karen had been helping Dad at the fairs since she was ten. It was fun at the beginning, working the snow cone machine, meeting the ride boys and gypsies, catching a glimpse of a giant man or a bearded woman. She'd even been introduced to one of the Flying Wallendas. At sixteen, it was the last place she wanted to be, but she had no other choice. Dad used all his vacation time to work the fairs and he needed her help. They would travel between Butler, Pennsylvania, and Canfield, Ohio, visiting several towns in between.

"Karen," Dad called from the hotdog truck. "Bring me another case of napkins."

Karen wrestled the box out the trunk of the car and lugged it into the truck. "Here you go," she said. They had arrived at 7:00 am with all the stock they'd need for the food trucks. Maud, a woman who had worked for them for years, showed up promptly as usual. She made chili for the hotdogs while Dad took inventory of the meat, buns, napkins, plates, and other items before putting them in their places.

You couldn't be too careful. One year one of the employees took some of their stock. Dad was always great with numbers. It didn't take him long to figure out things were missing. That was the end of that worker.

Dad poured oil into the fryer and wiped sweat from his forehead with his sleeve. To watch him in the morning, you'd think he was just another carney worker, a middle-age guy with thinning hair and a thickening belly. By the time the crowds arrived, he would be transformed. His eyes had an elfish sparkle. He'd start up a conversation with every customer, ask them where they were from, where they worked, how their day was going. All the time, he'd be sweating from the heat. His cheeks would be rosy. But he was in his element. He was the ring master of his own sideshow.

"Looks like we're ready here," Dad said. "Go on down and get the game booth set up. I'll have cash ready for you later."

"Okay," Karen said.

Karen wandered down the concourse. Leroy's Hot Sausages were already cooking. The spicy aroma wafting from his truck reminded her that she hadn't eaten breakfast. Steese's Ice Cream truck didn't have its windows open yet, but there was plenty of time to open before the 11:00 am start.

Their Birthday Game booth was down the concourse from Dad's other truck, between the Ring Toss and the Fishbowl. Just far enough that she could have some autonomy. After opening the booth and wiping down the playing area, she was free to wander the fair. Dad would be busy watching the French fryer and putting the hot dogs out to cook and never know she was gone.

One thing Karen enjoyed about the fair was all the color. Truck awnings and tents were a wonderful collection of stripes of every color combination. The grounds were awash in pink, yellow, orange, and blue. Stuffed animals hung from poles, waiting for winners to cart them home. Music blared. At night, it turned into an alien world of flashing lights, barkers luring people to their games, food aromas mingling and tempting all who passed by.

"Hey, Karen." Johnny, one of the ride boys, leaned against the metal gate to the Ferris wheel. "How's it goin'?"

"Fine," Karen said.

Johnny was a slim kid, not much older than her, with long blond hair and an ugly green mermaid tattoo on his left arm. He'd always been nice to her, but Mom would have a fit if she knew Karen was giving him the time of day. It's not that she had romantic interest in him, nor any of the ride boys. They weren't her type. She was going on to college, thinking of majoring in criminal justice, and maybe becoming a lawyer. She imagined defending Johnny in court one day.

Karen paused at the gate.

"Where you workin' this year?" he asked.

"The Birthday Game," she said. "Near my dad's truck." It was wise to remind the ride boys that she wasn't working alone. The threat of a dad being close by always helped keep them in line.

"Come on over later," he said. "I'll give you a ride."

"Sure. If we're not too busy." Thursdays were usually slow, but Dad didn't want her leaving the booth unattended during work hours. "I might see you later."

"Hey, did you see, the gypsies are here," he said. "Better watch your money."

"They're not like that, Johnny."

"You say that because you're friends with them."

"I'm friends with lots of people."

"Mike said they don't use their real names. Did you know that?" he said. "He said gypsies never tell their real name to people outside their family."

"Mike's crazy."

"No, it's the truth," Johnny said. "And they have a cleaning code. They wash shirts and pants separately."

At least they wash their clothes, Karen thought. She didn't think the ride boys washed very often. They always smelled of sweat and oil. Their hands were always black, especially around their fingernails. The gypsies, if that's what the traveling people really were, were impeccably clean.

"I've got to go," she said. "I'll see you later."

"What's your hurry?"

"Some of us have work to do."

"Sure," he said. "Me too." He stood upright, and she could feel him staring at her as she walked away. Some boys just couldn't take the hint.

Larry's Airbrush Art was set up around the corner from the Ferris wheel. Larry was usually a regular at the Canfield Fair. Karen was surprised to see his display here. The t-shirts were already hanging. Larry was behind them working on the side of a van.

Karen ducked between the shirts. "Hi, Larry," she said. "What are you doing here?"

Larry tipped back his black leather cap and smiled with the teeth he had left. He was skinnier than she remembered, and his long hair stringier. She wondered if he ever ate.

"Hey, Karen." He turned off the air compressor and pulled a cigarette from his pocket. "How ya doin'?" He motioned to the van. He'd painted part of a landscape with a castle and a dragon. "I told Vince I'd do his van for him."

"It looks great." She couldn't help being mesmerized by his work. She didn't know how he could just spray out a design like that. She'd seen him do portraits of all sorts of people. Someone could give him a photo, and in a little while they would have a portrait on a shirt. He was amazing.

Larry lit the cigarette and took a drag. "I'm pretty happy with it," he said. "You here with your dad?"

"He's doing foot-longs and fries," she said. "I'm running a game."

Larry blew smoke. "Send some people my way, will ya? Last time I came out here, I hardly made enough to pay for the gas. Got to make it worth my while."

"Sure," she said.

Larry took a final drag on the cigarette and tossed it to the ground. "Well, back to work. See you around, kid."

Beyond the food trucks, Karen spotted the gypsy camp. They had parked their trailers so close to each other they were almost touching. Johnny was right about one thing. The gypsies did stay to themselves most of the time. Today they were up to something special. A lamb roasted over a spit and picnic tables were lined in a row. Betty, the matriarch of the group, was shaking her finger while scolding a couple of younger boys. They stood with heads bowed.

Karen didn't want to bother her, but Betty noticed her before she turned away. She waved at Karen and walked to the edge of their encampment. Betty was short like Karen, but she had a confident stride that made her stand out in a crowd. Karen wasn't sure how old she was, but she kept her long hair tied back. This morning she wore matching turquoise capris and blouse and her usual compliment of rings, gold necklaces, and bangles.

"Hi, Karen," Betty said. "How's my favorite fair girl doing?"

"Okay," Karen said.

"You want to come in for a coke?"

Karen checked her watch. "Not today," she said. "I don't have time. Maybe tomorrow."

She'd visited with Betty in her trailer many times, but Mom and Dad had made it perfectly clear that she was not to be involved with fortune-telling or tarot cards. When she'd first met Betty, she'd thought that gypsies couldn't read. Maybe that was something her dad or one of the ride boys had told her. Just another rumor. If anyone could read, it was Betty. She not only knew how to interpret tarot cards, nothing got passed her. Not even Karen. No matter how normal Karen tried to be, she was sure Betty knew about the spirits, knew she was sensitive. But she never said a word.

Karen remembered the time she and Mom were watching a Harry Houdini movie with Tony Curtis. During a scene with a crystal ball, she'd told her mother, "I know I'm going to do that someday."

If Betty had been her mother, she would have handed her a crystal ball and said, "get to work, girl." As it was, Karen had decided to be a good Catholic, even going to mass on weekdays when she could.

"Make sure you stop to see the Pomona Grange ladies," Betty said. "They're making apple butter near my tent." Jewelry on her wrist jingled as she pointed toward the main concourse. "They have a big iron kettle over an open fire. Smells delicious."

"I'll do that," Karen said. The air was already filled with the aromas of hot sausage and popcorn at this end of the concourse. With no wind coming from the barns, that would be the only thing she smelled all day, thank goodness.

Karen took the long way around to pass by the fortune-telling tent. The Grange ladies were clad in colonial-style dresses, stirring their pot like a bunch of witches mixing a brew. Karen paused to watch them a moment, but her eyes kept drifting toward Betty's tent. Obie, God rest her soul, would have gone right in there. But Karen wasn't Obie. She didn't talk to spirits, didn't ask them questions, didn't encourage them in anyway. She hoped that someday they would be gone for good, and she wouldn't have to deal with them anymore.

"Come back this afternoon and we'll have samples ready," a Grange lady said.

Karen nodded and strolled to the main concourse. At the booth, she wiped down the front of the game. People had a habit of resting their drinks on the edge when they played. It could be a sticky mess by the end of the day. She thought about people trying to beat the odds, hoping their birthday would get called. Dad had assured her that the "house" always made money on the game. She should consider the profits part of her college savings.

Karen cleaned around each date and wondered about fortune-telling. It was just another way people tried to beat the odds. If they knew what their future held, they could cheat fate. In the end, she didn't think many were successful at changing their destiny. She imagined life as a large game, each person a piece trying to make their way around the board. What was her destiny? She saw herself being more like Mom, helping people in need, rather than Dad, who was the consummate showman. Whatever she became, it certainly wouldn't involve any mumbo-jumbo.

CHAPTER 10

NOVEMBER 1907: SPIRITUALISM COMES TO TOWN

Lydia watched people trickle into the rental hall. It was early November, but it felt as if it could snow at any moment. Many arrived bundled in hats and coats, which was just as well. The hall had a coal furnace, but the large room was far from warm.

Edward followed a group of women through the door and waved to Lydia. He slid sideways along a row of folding chairs. "It looks like it's going to be a good crowd," he said. "Reverend Brooks hasn't arrived yet?"

"No," Lydia said. "The Stansfields will be here with him soon."

"Are you introducing him?"

"I asked Alice if she would do the honor."

Alice had met Reverend Brooks at Lily Dale the previous year. She was the one who'd suggested he stop at New Castle after his visit with the First Spiritualist Church in Pittsburgh. Lydia didn't think it was a good idea at the time. After her trial, she was sure there wouldn't be enough people in the area to make his stop worthwhile. New Castle was a big city, but it wasn't ready for Spiritualism. It looked like she had been proven wrong.

A woman entered the hall in a tweed coat and brown fur hat. Mrs. Martin? Lydia squinted.

"What is it?" Edward asked.

"How dare she?"

"Who?" Edward glanced toward the doorway.

"It's Mrs. Martin. She's here. And it looks like two of the other women who testified against me are with her." Lydia's cheeks flushed. "They have a lot of nerve coming here."

"Pay no attention to them," Edward said. "There are plenty of others here seeking the truth. They are the ones who will benefit from Reverend Brooks's talk and demonstration."

Lydia tried not to watch but noticed that Mrs. Martin sat third row from the front. Was she hoping to get a reading from Reverend Brooks so she could refute it? Lydia didn't doubt she would try such a tactic.

"Look," Edward said, "the reverend has arrived."

Alice guided George H. Brooks across the back of the room. He was an unassuming sort of man. One wouldn't normally pick him out from the crowd. His suit was neither expensive nor well worn. He was graying about the temples, but he kept his hair trimmed short in the front as well as the back. Lydia thought he looked refreshed, considering this was his third day in New Castle. Alice had him on a fine-tuned schedule. The man was busy from morning until night. Even the dinner she and Edward had hosted for him had felt too rushed.

"I'm sorry we are running late," Alice said. "That old horse of ours hates this cold weather. She makes such a fuss sometimes. Poor William is probably having a time trying to get her to settle down out there. The place is a mad house."

"We have plenty of time," Lydia said. "Shall we get you up front, Reverend?"

"My pleasure," he said with a midwestern twang.

It wasn't long before the hall was awash in the din of conversation. Lydia noticed several of her clients in the crowd as well as the group from the Pittsburgh Spiritualist Church who had attended their smaller event two nights before. Ida Howard couldn't be missed in her overlarge fur coat as she entered the hall with supporters from the Youngstown church.

Alice Stansfield approached the podium. Her gray hair was pulled back from her face and she held a piece of paper before her. "Will everyone please be seated," she called out. Stragglers moved along the aisles taking the few seats that remained. The one hundred seats were filled. Lydia was astounded.

"I'd like to thank everyone for coming on this cold night," Alice said. "I will waste no more of your time and introduce the honorable Reverend George H. Brooks. Reverend Brooks is a member of the National Spiritualists Association and president of the Wisconsin State Spiritualists Association. He is a respected lecturer who has made public appearances for the past twenty years and has appeared in all of the largest cities on the public platform. He is a trance medium of the highest order. Whether you believe in Spiritualism or not, it is worthwhile to hear this man. He is considered one of the best platform speakers in the country." Alice moved back from the podium. "Without further ado, I introduce Reverend Brooks. His lecture tonight is entitled 'Spiritualism: What Is It?'"

The audience applauded. Mrs. Martin and her friends sat stone faced and unimpressed.

"Thank you for the wonderful welcome," Reverend Brooks said. "I can only ask that the spirits gathered with us from the other side warm your hearts."

Lydia gathered her skirts and sat on a folding chair at the end of the first row next to Alice and William. The crowd quieted.

"I will start at the beginning," Reverend Brooks said. "The story of Spiritualism begins with a small cabin in a rural town in western New York State. In December of 1847, John David Fox with his wife and two daughters, Catherine, twelve, and Margaretta, fifteen, moved into the Hydesville house. Before long, they found themselves frequently disturbed at night with the sounds as of furniture being moved or knocking on the doors and walls."

The crowd remained silent.

"On March 30, noises seemed to come from everywhere. Trying to figure out what was happening, Mr. Fox stood on one side of the door and his wife on the other, but the rappings seemed to emanate from the door between them. It became a sleepless night for the entire family. But like all nights, it was followed by the rising of the morning sun. What had been terrifying the night before, now seemed more like a mystery to solve.

"The next evening, Catherine tried to communicate with the mysterious spirit. She snapped her fingers and said, 'Here, old splitfoot, do as I do.' To everyone's surprise, the spirit responded with as many raps as she had snapped. Margaretta joined in, clapping her hands several times. 'Now do as I do,' she said. 'Count one, two, three, four.' The rappings correctly responded. And that is how communication with the spirit world began."

Lydia resisted the urge to look back at Mrs. Martin. She probably wasn't listening anyway. Old sour puss.

"When Mrs. Fox asked if it was human, it did not respond. But when she asked it to respond with two raps if I was spirit, it rapped twice distinctly. Through questions and answers, the family found that the spirit was that of a thirty-one-year-old man. At that moment, Ms. Fox suggested they call the neighbors to come witness the rapping. Mrs. Redfield, their next-door neighbor, came immediately. Mr. Redfield arrived thereafter and invited Mr. Duesler and several others to the house. A great many questions were asked of the spirit and answered correctly."

Reverend Brooks paused as if for dramatic effect. The audience remained engrossed.

"Mr. Duesler was the person who continued to question the mysterious entity about its demise. They eventually discovered that the subject had been murdered five years previously."

A commotion erupted in the center of the room. A man with a handlebar mustache stood and waved his hat. Lydia thought he might be trying to disrupt the speech.

"My wife," the man said. "She has fainted. Is there a doctor?" Alice nudged William. He went to the man's aid, and they helped the woman from the hall.

Reverend Brooks waited quietly.

"Sorry for the disruption," Alice said. "Please continue, Reverend Brooks."

"As I was saying," Reverend Brooks said, "once they discovered that the poor soul had been murdered, Mr. Duesler asked questions in relation to the murder. It was asked if different individuals had committed this murder until the perpetrator was identified as a man who had lived in the house several years previously. They continued their questioning and found that the man had been a peddler. The peddler's wife had died, but he still had children who were living. They were unsuccessful at trying to determine the dead man's name, only identifying two initials: C. and B. It was determined that he was buried in the cellar of the house."

A communal gasp echoed through the room.

"By this time, the rapping attracted hundreds of people, and none of the family was able to get any work done. Many excavations were made in the cellar, but no skeleton was ever found until three years ago, when bones were discovered by school students who were investigating part of the old cellar wall that had crumbled.

"After the initial events in Hydesville, Margaret and Catherine were sent to Rochester. Catherine went to the house of her sister Leah Fish, and Margaret to the home of their brother David. The rappings followed them. By 1849, they were giving public performances and the Spiritualist movement was born."

An hour later, Reverend Brooks reached the end of his lecture. Instead of taking questions, he invited Alice to conduct several readings while he took a short break, sitting on a chair near the podium. Lydia was impressed with Alice's skill. She would always begin with the name of the spirit and its relationship to a person in the crowd. Once the recipient of the message was identified, she would reveal additional information. One man was encouraged to seek a new job. A woman was assured by an aunt that she would conceive a child soon.

Reverend Brooks had appeared to be in prayer. At one point, his body jerked, and his breathing deepened. Lydia worried that he had fallen asleep.

"I have a Quentin," Alice said. "He was an uncle on the father's side of someone here. He passed as an old man from heart failure. Does anyone know this Quentin?"

No one responded.

Reverend Brooks rose from his chair with eyes closed. William moved forward, took him by the elbow, and helped him walk forward to the front row. Alice backed away.

"Is he in trance?" Edward whispered.

"I think so." Lydia had never seen a trance medium.

"I come here to bring hope," Reverend Brooks said in a voice quite a bit deeper than his own. "All darkness is removed. Life, love, and reason prevail. Put down all things that come between us. We are one."

The crowd sat at rapt attention. Even Mrs. Martin and her women friends seemed to be focused on Reverend Brooks's speech.

"Our world is very close to your own. Only death separates us," Brooks continued. He went on for several minutes, discussing his hope for the future of mankind. Then he grew quiet. Alice moved a chair behind him so he could sit. He returned to his sleep state for so long that a few at the rear of the audience got up and left.

When he spoke again, it was with an English accent. "Tell Dorothy that I understand," he said.

"Is there a Dorothy here?" William asked. Two women raised their hands.

"This is Johnny," Brooks said. "Johnny the father."

A woman in a black hat stood. Alice went to her, but Lydia couldn't hear what Alice said.

"It is time for you to return to the old homestead," Brooks said. "Do you follow me?"

"Yes," the woman said.

"You have been meaning to return, but you haven't. Some of the old places are still there. Even the old church where they took him. Can you hear me?"

Tears ran down the woman's face. "Yes," she stammered. "Yes, I can hear you."

"We have a fine place here," he said. "But you will not be here for many years."

Reverend Brooks continued with his readings well into the evening. Some people left, but most the crowd stayed the entire time. Lydia couldn't believe how positive the crowd's response was to Reverend Brooks. It had only been six months ago that she was in court defending her religious views. She hoped this would be a turning point for New Castle. Maybe Alice was right. Spiritualism could find a home in New Castle.

CHAPTER 11

JUNE 1970: COLLEGE IT IS

Karen's mom slid a meatloaf out of the oven. The pan banged against the stove top, and meaty-ketchup aroma enveloped their small kitchen. Karen arranged the kitchen nook table with their everyday dishes, gold-trimmed plates made right in town at Shenango China. She didn't mind helping with the housework, but now that she'd graduated from New Castle High School, she knew her parents would want her to find a job. She had always planned to go to college, but something held her back. She hadn't applied to any university, not even some of the local colleges. Now, it was summer, and she was caught in limbo between adolescence and adulthood.

When Aunt Tish recommended that she apply to Murphy's Department Store, she figured she might as well give it a try. At least she'd be making some money. That morning she'd walked downtown to the store on Washington Street. It didn't take long to fill out the application forms and take the math test. She was sure her parents would be happy that she was at least applying for a job. She could help pay her way like a responsible adult.

"Get the salad and dressing out of the fridge." Mom scooped mashed potatoes into a bowl.

Karen scooted around her and carefully opened the door. "We're out of Italian," she said.

"I'll have to add that to my list and stop at the store after work tomorrow."

"I can go to the store tomorrow," Karen said.

Mom chuckled. "I keep forgetting that you are out of school," she said. "Have you read that booklet on Youngstown State?"

"I looked at it." She placed the salad and dressings in the middle of the table. They'd have to use Thousand Island or French tonight.

"You're going to have to make up your mind about college soon. It's June already."

"I know," Karen said.

Attending college would be fine if there was a particular occupation that excited her. She wasn't much interested in teaching or nursing. She'd been thinking about criminal justice, but she was really drawn to parapsychology. As hard as she'd worked to seem normal, she couldn't stop her attraction to psychic phenomena. It was a ridiculous idea. You couldn't get a job in that subject, or at least she thought so until she'd found Duke University.

"Go get your father," Mom said. "I think he's checking the tire on the car."

Karen went down the steps to the side door, pushed open the screen door, and glanced at the cars in the driveway. "Dad?" She didn't see him. "Dad!"

"I'm down here," he called from the basement.

"It's time for dinner."

"I'll be right up."

It didn't take Dad long to take his seat at the table. He was a no-nonsense kind of man and a no-nonsense eater. Karen hardly had her salad on her plate when he was digging into hefty helpings of meat and potatoes. Despite Mom's complaints that he needed to eat more vegetables he was strictly nonvegetarian. To keep her happy, he added a small portion of salad.

"Did you get the tire fixed?" Mom asked him.

"Yep."

"How was work today?"

"You know. Same old, same old." He shrugged and chewed. "Did Bob Aldridge show up at the clinic?"

"You know I can't tell you that." Mom thought it was important to maintain a nurse-patient privilege at the shop. She said there was enough gossip going on at Rockwell without her adding to it.

"Well, he better have showed up." Dad gulped down a large wad of potatoes. "The guy's always making excuses. He's sick. He cut his hand. Either that or I find him out back having a smoke. He's going to get fired if he keeps it up. You just can't find good help these days."

"Speaking of work, I have good news," Karen said. "I went down to Murphy's today and put in an application. Aunt Tish is sure I'll be hired."

Dad paused with a forkful of meatloaf halfway to his mouth. "Aunt Tish," he said. "I told her to stay out of this. I'm not having you settle for a low-wage job working in a department store."

Karen's stomach suddenly felt full. "But I thought you'd be happy I was looking for work."

"You can work at the fair," Dad said. "Then start college this fall."

Karen felt her cheeks grow warm. She'd already had this conversation with him more times than she could count. She didn't want another argument.

"We've been saving for years for you to go to college," he said. "You need more than a job. You need a career. You're not going to have a career working at a dead-end job. You need an education." She had college-educated cousins on both sides of the family. Some of them had full-ride scholarships. Dad took pride in the fact that he came from intelligent stock.

"Your father's right, honey," Mom said. "You have to support yourself economically. There are plenty of things for you to study in college. How about nursing?"

Nursing. Nursing. Nursing. Karen slammed her fork on the table more forcefully than she expected.

"I don't want to be a nurse." How many times did she have to tell Mom that? She'd thought about being a nurse like Mom when she was a kid. But now, she was sure she wasn't cut out for that job. Handling blood and bodily fluids was gross. She didn't know how Mom did it every day.

"What about teaching?" Dad said. "Business. Accounting."

Karen stared at her lap. Maybe she should be honest with them and tell them what her true interest was.

"You don't have to make up your mind right away," Mom said. "Start with some general courses. Then you can decide on a major."

Dad finished his meatloaf and helped himself to a second piece. "You're going to college this fall, come hell or high water. Major or not."

Karen knew they were right. A college education was better than a job at Murphy's. But why should she study something she had no interest in?

"I was thinking about majoring in parapsychology."

Her dad chewed.

"What kind of psychology is that?" Mom asked.

"It's a new area of study," Karen said. "They research ESP and psychic phenomena."

Dad swallowed. "You've got to be kidding me," he said.

"I've checked it out," Karen said. "UCLA and Duke University have parapsychology labs."

"Sounds like something a bunch of pot-smoking hippies would do," he said. "And what are you going to do with a *degree* in parapsychology? Fortune-telling at the fair? I knew I shouldn't have let you make friends with those gypsies."

"It's not like that," Karen said. "There's a Dr. Rhine at Duke University who's studying ESP and consciousness. There's even an Academy of Parapsychology and Medicine."

Dad shook his head. "This was your grandmother's doing. Filling your head with fairy stories."

He was right. Obie would understand. Wee People. Spirits. ESP. Karen considered telling Dad that spirits lived in this very house. If she wanted to, she could sense them any time she wanted. That was probably the last thing Dad wanted to hear. She held her tongue.

"It's a type of psychology, Dad," she said. "They're doing research."

"I don't care what they call it," he said. "You're going to pick a traditional major, something that will lead to a good job. I don't want to hear anything else about this ESP nonsense."

"Fine." Karen grabbed her dishes and slid from her seat. He couldn't make her go to college. Just let him try. She would fail all her classes. Then he'd regret sending her.

She grabbed a bottle of dish soap from the counter and turned the water on full force, watching bubbles fill the sink. Lemon scent wafted into the air.

"College. This fall," Dad said. "And if you don't register, I'll do it for you."

"Don't worry," Mom said. "She'll take care of it in her own time."

"She's had plenty of time," he grumbled.

Karen washed the potato pot, her dish and silverware, and placed them in the drainer. Instead of letting the meatloaf pan soak, she scrubbed and scrubbed until Dad excused himself from the table and went outside. Mom brought the other dishes to the sink.

"Your dad just wants what is best for you," she said. "We want you to be independent and able take care of yourself. Your father and I will be gone someday, and we want to make sure you have the right tools and skills."

Karen scrubbed some more. Mom waited quietly.

Karen took dishes from her and let them sink into the sudsy water. How was she supposed to explain what she felt? She remembered that day on the operating table like it was yesterday. Were the tunnel and the spirit people she'd seen only a dream? Was there something wrong with her? Maybe she was crazy. Maybe this fascination with ESP and clairvoyance was part of the craziness.

"Why don't we go over to Youngstown State on my day off?" Mom said. "The campus isn't very far. You can live at home and commute. It won't be so bad. You'll meet some new friends and take some interesting classes."

Karen chased the silverware around the bottom of the sink.

"We can check out the psychology department," Mom said. "Psychology is a good field."

"What if I don't like it?" Karen rinsed the silverware.

"You won't know until you've tried."

Maybe going to college would be best for her. She would get an education, find a normal job, make lots of money, and save it. Then, when she was well situated, she would quit her job and go into parapsychology. "Okay," Karen said. "I'll try it."

Karen felt the tension lift. It was as if the house gave an audible sigh of relief. Had the spirits been waiting for her to make this decision? If so, what was she supposed to do with her life now?

CHAPTER 12

OCTOBER 1908: RIGHT TO WORSHIP

Lydia and Edward followed the crowd out of the Cascade Vaudeville into the dimly lit city. It was still raining, although not as heavily as when they entered. Edward waited until they crossed the trolley tracks lining the middle street and the throng thinned before opening the umbrella. Lydia held a handkerchief over her nose and ducked under cover.

"It's getting cold," she said as they walked to Washington Street where the streetlights were brighter.

"Your lungs aren't bothering you, are they?"

"No," she said. It was usually dust and smoke that brought on an attack, but cold would sometimes set off an incident. She couldn't be too careful.

"It's all my fault for bringing you to this dirty city," he said.

"It's not like you had a choice," she said. "You have a good job with the railroad."

"But you didn't have to come with me," he said. "We are not bound by marriage. You could ..."

"Hush," she said. "We are life partners. Having a piece of paper makes no difference to me."

"But I ..."

"No more talk of that," she said. A trolley rushed by, splashing water on the sidewalk ahead of them. The hem of her dress was soaked, and she could feel the wetness creeping up her stockings. "I think we should try the Coliseum the next time we go out. I heard that they have a band and a juggler."

"It would be a nice change," he said. "Or we could go to the Bom-Bay. The guys at work say the Ericksons are good."

They waited for a horse and buggy to pass before crossing the street. Ahead, the Pearson Building loomed like a medieval castle. The stone and conical towers looked ominous in the darkness. Two windows glowed amid the darkness, like golden eyes.

"We shouldn't have gone out in this weather," Edward said. "You will catch your death of cold."

"You worry too much," Lydia said. She wouldn't admit to him that was one of his endearing qualities.

"Isn't that William Stansfield ahead?"

A man was exiting the Pearson Building, trailing a large crowd of people. Lydia couldn't see his face beneath his hat rim, but she recognized the black wool coat and goulashes. "Yes, that's William."

They had seen him just over a week ago at the memorial services for Emily, wife of his son, Samuel. Yesterday morning, they heard the devastating news that the baby had died also. The passing of a child is a great blow, even to a Spiritualist. You can try to tell yourself that the young life was not wasted, that spirit guides would be waiting for it when it crossed. That still didn't stop the pain of the loss.

"William!" Edward called out as they crossed North Street to Neshannock Avenue.

William turned his attention from a couple who accompanied him. "Edward," he said. "Lydia. What are you doing out this time of the evening?"

"We're on our way back from the Cascade," Edward said. "And you?"

"I had a talk to give at the Unity Club tonight," he said. "Desultorium: the issues of life, materiality, and spirituality."

"After your rebuke to Dr. Roark in the paper last week, I'm sure Spiritualism is on the lips of everyone in town," Edward said. "It looks like you had a fairly large audience."

"Not bad for such an evening." He looked to the sky. "I must say, weather like this reminds me of England."

Lydia nudged Edward. He nudged her back.

Lydia removed the hanky from her mouth and cleared her throat. "We want to give our condolences," she said. "We heard about the death of the baby."

William nodded. "Thank you," he said. "Some things cannot be helped. But I take solace in knowing that the child is with Emily in the world beyond."

"Of course," Lydia said.

Annie, Charley whispered. *It begins.*

Lydia turned her attention to the couple standing with William. The man was thin, almost gaunt. His hands were stained black, probably from working at the mill. The woman wore glasses and her red hair peeked out from below a wide-brimmed hat.

"I'm sorry," William said. "I am being remiss. Let me introduce you to the—"

"Daniel Johns," the man said with a thick brogue. He extended his hand. "And my wife, Annie."

"This is Edward and Lydia Marquette," William said.

"*The* Lydia Marquette?" Annie asked. "From the fortune-teller trial?"

"I'm a Spiritualist," Lydia said. She hoped people weren't going to identify her as a fortune-teller for the rest of her life. It had been over a year. How long would she be known as the woman who went to trial? She could only hope her stained reputation would pass with time.

Annie laughed. "Oh, I know that," she said. "Being cut from the same cloth."

Lydia couldn't quite understand the woman because of the thick accent.

"In Wales, they say we speak to the fey," she said. "But it's not truly that. We speak to those on the other side, those who have passed before. Is that not so?"

"Yes," Lydia said.

"Then we be one and the same," she said. "I have read of your Fox sisters of New York and the ones who came after. It appears the new Spiritualism is pitted against old Christianity. I find it odd that those who tout a belief in heaven and the afterlife are first to condemn those of us to speak with those who have passed."

"That is why we attended Mr. Stansfield's talk," Daniel said. "We have lived in the city for a while, but were looking for kindred spirits, so to speak. We think it's important that people understand the true meaning of Spiritualism. As Mr. Stansfield stated, it is purely materialism that is keeping the avenues closed, and the churches should be natural allies of opening the way of knowledge to the darkened spiritual vision. Alas, they are not."

"Edward and I have been debating the issue since before the trial," Lydia said. "Pittsburgh has its own Spiritualist Church. Edward was a representative at a meeting created to establish the state organization in February. We had a remarkably successful medium demonstration November last with Reverend Brooks from Wisconsin, but the local ministers are still speaking out against Spiritualism, calling us frauds and shysters."

"They don't understand that the Bible is full of Spiritualism," William said. "If Reverend Martin would have been with Jesus at the well of Samaria, when he told the woman various events in her life, he would have hauled Jesus away to the city hall, or some other place of confinement."

Lydia shivered. "Our house is just up Neshannock Avenue," she said. "Would you like to stop in for a cup of tea? Or a nightcap?"

William checked his pocket watch. "I am an abstainer," he said. "Besides, it's getting late, and I have a trolley to catch."

"We would be happy to join you for a wee nip," Annie said.

The rain was coming down in earnest when they reached the front porch. Edward shook off the umbrella and motioned for the women to enter. "After you, ladies."

Lydia removed her dripping coat and helped Annie remove hers. There would be a mess in the entryway in the morning. "Please, have a seat in the parlor," she said. "I'll get us something to drink."

The only hard liquor they had in the cupboard was some Old Crow bourbon that she mostly used to make cough remedies, and a bottle of sloe gin someone had given Edward. Lydia searched the cupboard for matching glasses and carried them into the parlor on a tray with the bottle.

"I hope this will do," she said, placing the tray on the table. What?" Annie said. "No Irish whiskey?"

"Sorry."

Annie laughed.

Edward poured them each a shot. "I'm afraid the only good spirits you'll get in this house are from the other side," he said.

"We've become accustomed to the bad beer and whiskey here in America."

Edward held his glass high. "To new friends," he said.

More than friends, Charley whispered.

"New friends," everyone repeated.

Annie and Daniel gulped their drinks, and Edward refilled the glasses. Lydia took only a sip, but the heat filled her chest and lungs.

"So," Lydia said, "do you work as a medium, Annie?"

"Not since we've come here," she said. "I cannot take the chance of getting arrested. Danny's working at the mill. We got wee ones at home to care for."

"I don't think the authorities will try to arrest another medium anytime soon," Edward said. "Alice Stansfield has been advertising in the paper without recourse."

"And they haven't even tried to investigate the Great Hindoo, who is an obvious shyster," Lydia added. "In his advertisements, he calls himself a professor and states he is a trance medium, healer, and advisor. He even claims to be an astrologer and phrenologist."

"You have no fear of the authorities?" Daniel said.

"I feel I am a person whose faith, belief, and ideas come under the head of Spiritualism," Lydia said. "As a Spiritualist, I shall exercise the right to worship as I please, which is a right that is given and ensured to me by our federal Constitution."

"Here. Here." Daniel raised his glass. "To the spirit world."

"To the spirit world."

CHAPTER 13

APRIL 1971: SHE WAS NORMAL

Karen recognized the sound of Rod Heasley's old '65 Plymouth Fury from a block away. It had a solid rumble that reminded her of Rod. He had a steady way about him and was singularly focused on life. Things that would normally upset her, he took in stride. He was the ground to her sky, the rock to her water. Maybe that's what attracted her to him. That, and his good looks.

She glanced in the mirror to make sure her curls were under control. Rod wasn't the type to be concerned about her appearance, but this was date night. She wanted to look nice.

"Karen," Mom called from downstairs. "Rod is here."

"I know," Karen said. She grabbed her sweater and purse from the bed and flung the strap over her shoulder. A knock on the front door echoed up the stairs. Karen rushed down. At six feet tall, Rod filled the doorway.

"Hey," he said through the screen, brushing back long bangs from his round face. "You ready to go?"

"Yeah." Karen turned. "See ya later, Mom."

"Hi, Rod." Mom walked into the living room, drying her hands on a dish towel. "Where are you going tonight?"

"A movie." Karen opened the door. Rod looked nice with tan striped pants and button-down shirt, but Mom looked worried. Karen didn't think she'd be happy with any boy she brought home. Mom was too protective.

"Don't be out too late," Mom said.

"We won't."

Karen stepped onto the porch.

"Be careful."

"We will."

The evening was warm for April. Karen followed Rod to the car. He opened the door for her like an old-fashioned gentleman. Karen slid onto the bench seat. Rod worked in the bakery at Joseph's Supermarket, and the car's interior always smelled sweet, like cake and donuts.

"*Love Story* is playing at the Hi-Lander," Karen said.

"I was afraid you were going to say that." Rod closed the door, circled around the back of the car, and opened the driver's door.

"You don't want to see it?"

"Hmm."

Rod started the car and threw it into drive. The radio sprang to life, partway through "Jesus Christ Superstar."

"We can see something else," Karen said. "But everybody says it's a great movie."

"Yeah," Rod turned onto Croton Avenue and coasted down the hill to the traffic light.

"We don't have to see it."

"No," he said. "It's okay."

"You sure?" She spent every week at Youngstown State working through their criminal justice program, sometimes doing twelve-hour days. Rod had National Guard training one weekend a month, so their time together was limited. She'd been looking forward to seeing the movie, but she was flexible.

"It's fine," he said. "Next time, I get to pick the movie though."

"It's a deal," she said. As long as it wasn't a war movie. She was sick of seeing Vietnam on TV every night. Her boyfriend before Rod had been drafted. He never talked about his tour of duty when he came back home. People said that because he was small, he'd worked as a tunnel rat. Rats were sent into tunnels to kill the Vietcong and plant explosives. The enemy would lie in wait for them and tunnels could be booby-trapped. He wasn't the same person after he came home.

Rod didn't have a high draft number, but it was a constant worry that he'd be called up next. When he suggested that he join the National Guard, Karen wasn't happy. There was still the chance that he might be deployed to Nam. Rod decided it was the best choice for him. He spent six months training at Fort Dix, but at least when he returned home, he was the same old Rod.

Karen didn't know what was worse, dying or coming back so changed you'd never live a normal life. She thought of all those dying boys. Did they go through the dark tunnel when they died out in the jungle? Or was her childhood memory just her imagination? Catholics believed in Saint Peter and the pearly gates. Purgatory. And Hell. She still tried to be a good Catholic.

Traffic slowed to a crawl as they entered the downtown. Saturday nights were usually busy, but this evening was exceptionally so. They turned on Mill Street and headed up the hill. John Lennon's "Instant Karma" played on the radio. Karen found herself humming along. She'd been a Beatles fan since she first saw them on the *Ed Sullivan Show*. She knew the words to every song and had every one of their records. Her only regret was not being able to see them in concert when she was in eighth grade. She still couldn't forgive her dad for not allowing her to go to Cleveland with her friends. Now the Beatles were broken up. She enjoyed their solo songs, but it wasn't the same.

In the time it took to find a parking place and get tickets, all the good theater seats were taken. They sat so close to the front, Rod slid down in the seat to keep from blocking people's view.

The movie was slow at first, but Karen couldn't help but like Oliver and Jenny. Theirs was a modern-day Romeo and Juliette story. Forbidden love. Jenny's hospital death was gut wrenching. Karen couldn't hold the tears back. She reached for tissues in her purse and hoped Rod didn't notice. He'd tease her the rest of the night.

A later scene opened in the cemetery and she was sure she heard a sniffle from Rod. The old softy. He would never admit he'd teared up during a romantic movie, but she loved him even if he didn't let his soft side show.

"The movie was pretty good," Karen said as they exited the

theater and squeezed between cars in the lot. "Don't you think?"

"It was okay." Rod shrugged.

"A real tear-jerker."

"Yeah." Rod opened the door for her. "I don't know how you can enjoy all those *Twilight Zone* and *Chilly Willy* shows and still want to watch all this sappy stuff."

"I can like more than one thing, Rod."

"I suppose."

"Speaking of the *Twilight Zone*," Karen said. "I talked to Vera the other day. She said they can show us where that haunted tree is."

"You mean the Amish boy's ghost?" Vera's husband, Ed, had told Rod the story. Two Amish boys had been out hunting and one of the boys accidently shot and killed the other. The dead boy's ghost was said to travel through the trees with a lantern near the location where he was shot.

"Yeah," Karen said. "It's still early. We could stop at their apartment and see if they're home."

"Sure," Rod said. "Why not." He slammed the car door.

Rod cut through the neighborhoods, past craftsman-style houses with their wide front porches, boxy two-story four-squares lined up in neat rows, and a few fancier Tudor-style homes. Ed and Vera's apartment was on Blaine Street. The lights were on in the old house. Rod parked the car out front and let it idle.

"I'll see if they want to go," Karen said. She buttoned up her sweater and followed the sidewalk to the porch, climbed the steps, and knocked on the screen door. The TV played faintly inside.

Vera opened the inner door and greeted Karen with a wide smile. Her long blond hair was tied back in a ponytail. A flowered blouse hung over her bell-bottom jeans.

"Hey, Karen," she said. "What's up?"

"Not much. Rod and I just went to see *Love Story*. We were thinking about taking a drive to see the place where the Amish boy died. I thought you guys might want to show us where it's at."

"Sure," Vera said. "We were just watching *Bonanza*. I'll get

Ed."

Karen returned to the car. "Bridge over Troubled Waters" and "Let It Be" played on the radio as they waited. She was beginning to think Ed didn't wanted to give up watching *Bonanza* when the two of them bounded down the front steps. Ed climbed into the backseat after Vera. She laughed and slid behind Karen. "I can't believe you haven't gone up there yet," Vera said. "You won't believe it."

"The strangest thing I've ever seen," Ed said. In the dim radio light, his mustache cast a long shadow over his mouth so that his voice seemed disembodied.

Rod made a U-turn on Blaine and stepped on the gas. "It's out Route 18, isn't it?"

"Yeah," Ed said.

They took the road north to Maitland Lane. Vera sang along with "War" by the Temptations. Rod looked a bit embarrassed. Karen decided not to join in but couldn't keep from humming along.

Maitland was considered part of the city, but trees lined most of the road and the houses were far enough apart that it felt like countryside. Dark shadows hung over them, and the Plymouth rumbled through the night like it was the only car for miles. At the intersection with Route 18, Rod turned right and headed out of town into the dark countryside.

They passed the Apple Castle building with its artificial crenulations and oversized apple sign. Fruit trees on each side of the road were just starting to leaf out. Karen held her wrist near the dashboard lights and checked her watch for the time. It was after ten. "How late was it when you saw it last time?"

"I don't know," Vera said. "Late."

An orange triangle reflected off the rear of an Amish buggy on the road ahead. Rod slowed and pulled into the oncoming lane to pass. Karen glimpsed a family with two small children inside, Mom clad in black bonnet and dress, Dad wearing a straw hat.

"We'll have to look out for cops," Ed said. "I think they hide up there and wait for people to stop. I can't believe they gave us a ticket."

"What else were you doing in the car?" A little smile crept over Rod's face. Vera laughed.

"If I was going to make out, I sure wouldn't have done it in the middle of the road," Ed said.

"The turn is coming up," Vera said. "There. By that brick house."

Rod slowed the car. They turned off the main highway onto a dirt road lined with fields. The car bumped over several ruts. "The Long and Winding Road" played. Rod turned down the music. It was a clear cool evening, but it suddenly felt damp and heavy. Karen's skin prickled.

"There!" Vera said. "Those two trees."

Rod slowed the car to a crawl. The old maples were tall and wide, their craggy bark cracked and gouged over the years. Long branches intertwined over the road, creating an arbor of branches. In the golden glow of the car's headlights, they almost appeared to be in motion, reaching for each other.

"Stop here," Ed said. "Spirit in the Sky" played quietly on the radio.

Rod glanced in the rearview mirror and stopped the car. "I don't see any cops sneaking up," he said.

Vera leaned forward and rested her chin on the front seat. She pointed left. "The light starts over there," she said. "Then moves to the other tree."

Rod shut off the car and rolled down his window. Karen scanned the darkness. The surrounding fields were eerily quiet. There were no distant sounds of traffic, no wind rustling leaves, no insects chirping, no mammals scratching in the ditches. They sat still five, ten minutes. Nothing.

"There!" Rod said. A white light appeared amid the tree's leaves. "Do you see it?"

"Yes," Karen whispered.

"That's it!" Vera said.

"Do you think it's a ghost?" Rod asked.

"They say he doesn't know he's dead," Vera said. "He's wandering with a lantern, looking for a way home."

Karen felt a familiar pressure along her breastbone. A spirit was here. She was sure of it. Why had she wanted to come here? She worked so hard to be normal. Going to church. Getting good grades in college. This was the last thing she needed to be doing, but she couldn't help herself.

"Maybe this is only a farmhouse light or a car in the distance," Rod said. "A trick of the light."

"It's some trick if it is," Vera said.

No trick, Karen thought. If it was a boy wandering among the trees, he wasn't looking for a way home. She was sure of that. The spirits in her room didn't seem to be searching for anything or trapped on the Earth. Maybe the boy was trying to communicate something. She'd never spoken with the spirits in her room.

She tried to concentrate. *Are you here, little boy? Are you trying to tell us something?*

"There. It just moved," Vera said. "Did you see that?"

"Yeah," Rod said. "This is strange."

Karen breathed deeply. *I'm here, little boy. I don't know what you're trying to say._*

"I have to admit," Rod said, "I thought you were pulling my leg, Ed."

"Have I ever lied to you?" Ed said.

Rod chuckled. The light flickered as it moved among the branches.

"I've never seen anything like it." Rod looked at Karen. "Have you?"

Karen didn't dare answer.

"Car!" Ed said.

Rod looked at the rearview mirror. White light reflected onto his face. "Shit." He started the car and put it in drive. The car lurched forward. Vera fell backward. Karen grasped the door handle to keep from tumbling.

"Do you think it's the cops?" Rod asked.

"I don't know," Ed said. "Just keep going. But don't speed."

"That's easy for you to say." Rod backed off on the gas. The car behind them stayed at a distance. "Whose crazy idea was it to go ghost hunting?"

Karen stared out the side window across the dark fields.

Crazy. Is that what she was? Would she ever be able to tell Rod about the spirits who had visited her as a child? And if she told him that, could she also tell him about leaving her body and seeing the dark tunnel. Rod was laid-back, but she wasn't sure how he'd accept her real self. He was a normal guy. If she told him, maybe he would decide she was too strange to date. Would he want to marry a woman who could see spirits? She didn't think so. No. There was no way she could mention any of this.

CHAPTER 14

SEPTEMBER 1911: A CHURCH

Lydia stepped from the trolley onto the Long Avenue sidewalk. It was another hot and humid afternoon. To the west, the Tin Mill belched smoke and noise, its ever-present darkness dropping a layer of soot over buildings large and small. Fisher's Big Store loomed before her. It was no coincidence that the trolley stopped right at their front door. Lydia couldn't help but gaze at the window displays. Dress gingham, eight cents a yard. Ladies skirts, a dollar twenty-five. Men's full suits for fifteen dollars. Edward needed a new suit, especially since he was now a representative for the railroad line, but it seemed they never had any extra money.

She covered her mouth with a handkerchief to keep out the worst of the soot and walked past narrow, two-story shotgun houses. Daniel and Annie's house was a couple of blocks east of the mill, but that made no difference. Their clapboard might have been painted white at some point in time, but it was gray now, like all the others.

Every step leading up to the front porch squealed under Lydia's high-heeled shoes. A dog behind one of the houses barked a warning but didn't come to the front. She knocked on the edge of the screen door and peered inside. The living room, furnished with an overstuffed chair and a sofa that had seen better days, sat in afternoon shadow. The adjoining dining room held a dining table stacked with red and yellow jars of canned tomatoes and hot peppers. The only part of the kitchen visible from the front door was the stove. It held a steaming pot.

"Hello," Lydia called.

Annie appeared from the kitchen, wiping her hands on an apron stained with tomato juice.

"I knew ya'd be by." Annie unlatched the door and motioned for her to step inside. Without pausing, she made her way back to the kitchen.

"Don't tell me you're claiming to be a psychic now," Lydia said.

Annie laughed. "I didn't need to use my talents to know you'd be coming by," she said. "As soon as I heard the Stansfields were moving, I knew you'd be hot under the collar."

"You know me too well." She wasn't really mad at the Stansfields. It was the situation.

Lydia removed her hat and followed Annie. Her reading table was tucked into a corner of the dining room next to the stairs. She insisted she needed no help reaching the spirit world, but always used a lit candle to enable the spirits to find her. Lydia was a bit resentful. Charley was usually cooperative, but she felt it would be better if she could work directly with the spirits.

Annie's daughter, Agnes, was busy at the kitchen sink pealing skins off tomatoes. She was a younger version of her mother, though she did have Daniel's long, thin nose. At seventeen, she was already an accomplished medium. According to Annie, if it wasn't for her shyness, she would be wowing the crowds up at Lily Dale.

"William says they are moving to be near their son." Lydia rolled up her sleeves and joined Agnes at the sink. "But I think it's this stubborn town. William's been our most vocal proponent for Spiritualism. Where would we be if he wasn't here to write all those editorials to the news."

"In jail with the Great Hindoo," Annie said.

"If anyone needed to be put in jail for swindling, it was him," Lydia said. "I couldn't believe Mrs. Mack paid him ninety dollars for a prediction on a lucky ticket. It was partly her fault for being so gullible."

"I couldn't agree more," Annie said. "But we must continue on. Without William and Alice, we must take over the fight."

"That is easier said than done," Lydia said. She popped a tomato from its skin and passed it to Agnes to cut.

"Reverend Martin transferred to Ohio," Annie said. "And the last time Reverend Higley publish an editorial in the paper, they ran that letter from the Wampum man who spoke up for Spiritualism. Things are changin'."

"Maybe you're right," Lydia said. "But what are we going to do without Alice helping us make connections? And who is going to represent us at the Ohio Convention of Spiritualists?"

"A church," Agnes said in almost a whisper. She glanced at Lydia with calm green eyes. Lydia let her tomato slip back into the sink. A shiver of fear traveled through her.

"What did you say?" Lydia said.

"A church," Agnes repeated.

"What church?"

"Our church," Annie said. An amused smile crossed her face. Lydia felt a flutter of anxiety in her stomach. Alice had suggested several times that they have a medium come from Youngstown or Lily Dale to do more demonstrations. But a church? Impossible.

Annie chuckled. "A Spiritualist church would shake things up, wouldn't it?"

"A little too much," Lydia said. "I think we should just invite guest mediums to town. A church is too much to ask for."

"I'm not sayin' we build a brick-and-mortar church," Annie said. "Why not rent a hall?"

"And who would attend this church? Don't forget, it was God-fearing, *church*-attending women who were ready to hang me a few short years ago."

Annie's daughter, Mabel, almost as old as Agnes, came in the back door with a clothes basket on one hip and her two-year-old brother, Raymond, on the other. "Clothes are hung," she said. "Ray's fussing. I'm putting him down for his nap."

"I need you to help with the rest of this canning," Annie said.

Mabel rolled her eyes and tramped out of the room.

"We can bring Reverend Brooks back," Lydia said. "His talk brought in a lot of people, but I think most came out of curiosity. If we are going to bring together like-minds, I think we should have a smaller gathering. Something more like the Unity Club meetings that William attends. Just for those with an honest interest in Spirituality. We can have someone speak about Spiritualism. How mediumship works. How to identify a shyster."

Lydia stripped the last tomato of its skin. She remembered the scowl on Mrs. Martin's face at the end of the trial. She was ready to imprison Lydia for fortune-telling, and here they were, a few short years later planning a Spiritualist church in the city. The old biddy would spontaneously combust at the idea.

"We'll still need to rent a place to have a meeting," Annie said.

"Not if we meet in someone's house."

Annie wiped her hands on a towel. "We certainly can't meet here," she said. "Unless you plan on having only six people."

"You and Danny need to move out of this neighborhood," Lydia said. "Come up to Neshannock Avenue."

"I'm not the one keeping us from the move," she said. "Danny likes being close to the mill. He can walk to work in ten minutes from here."

"Tell him it's for Spiritualism. You have important work to do."

Annie chuckled. "No one knows better than Danny that I do my work anywhere," she said. "Sometimes I have trouble keeping the spirits at bay. My mind's *too* open to the other side, he says."

"Can't say I have that problem," Lydia said. "I guess I rely on Charley too much."

"We all work in different ways," Annie said. "Back home, I knew mediums who had such a clear connection with the spirit world, you would have thought they were talking with the spirits over the phone."

Agnes passed two tomato-filled jars fitted with caps to her mother. Holding them by the neck, Annie lowered them into the steaming pot.

"Back to the idea of a church," Annie said.

"Meeting," Lydia said. "Let's start with a small group. I'll talk to some of my clients. We can meet at my house. Then if there is enough interest, we'll discuss bringing in someone to speak."

"Maybe we can get Ida Howard from Youngstown to speak. She *has* a Spiritualist church."

"I'm not saying we should never have a church," Lydia said. "I'm just saying we should start small."

"The first step," Agnes said. Her attention focused out the kitchen window as if she were admiring the maples gone gold and red with the season. Agnes's hands trembled. Her eyes closed.

"Agnes?" Lydia said.

"I told you," Annie whispered. "She has a gift greater than mine."

Agnes sank into a chair by the table. Her mouth gaped open and her breath slowed.

"Who's here?" Annie asked.

"Mrs. Bushnell." Agnes's voice was deeper and older. "I am Mrs. Bushnell."

Steam erupted from the canning pot, filling the kitchen. Lydia backed away, shocked.

"I bring greetings from the spirit world." Three raps echoed through the room. "In the second state after death, I am now aware of the deeper parts of my inner nature. I am here to guide you. To assure you. These things must pass."

There'd been plenty of advertisements at Lily Dale touting physical phenomenon. This was the first time Lydia had witnessed it. Mrs. Bushnell was able to reach more readily through the curtain between worlds.

"Time is an ever-cycling phenomenon," Mrs. Bushnell continued. "What are years to you, are moments to us."

Canning jars rattled in the pot. "People will come. In the blink of an eye."

"To the church?" Annie whispered.

"Yes," Mrs. Bushnell said. "Be ready."

Agnes took a deep breath and opened her eyes. She glanced down at her hands. "Did it happen again?"

"Yes, dear," Annie said. She looked at Lydia. "You see. We are to start a church. Like it or not."

CHAPTER 15

MAY 1977: NEAR-DEATH EXPERIENCE

Karen couldn't keep from yawning. She hoped Dr. Greenman didn't notice. He was an aging hippy, a short man with glasses and salt-and-pepper hair who rode his bike to class. He was also one of her favorite instructors, and she liked his existential philosophy class. The idea that humans defined their own meaning in life was refreshing, especially after being brought up Catholic, where all meaning was decided and written in stone, no questions asked.

Best of all, she liked that he didn't believe in tests. Instead, he had his students write their thoughts in a journal during the semester. He said he didn't want to restrict their ability to develop their own thoughts. Tests forced them to respond to the instructor's ideas, not have their own.

"Remember, Nietzsche believed every great person has a collection of values," Dr. Greenman said. "Groups of people create values, but it's acting on those shared values that makes them successful."

Karen's stomach growled. It was almost nine and she'd skipped dinner. She hoped Rod hadn't finished off the leftover pizza. She didn't feel like cooking for herself when she got home.

Dr. Greenman held up a white paperback with red and orange cover colors. "Your assignment for next week is to read *Life after Life* by Raymond Moody. It's a fast read, and will be quite a departure from Nietzsche, but I think you'll find it interesting. We'll discuss the first two chapters, so come prepared. See you next week."

Karen shoved her notebook into her over-full backpack and followed the crowd from the classroom. Most of the students were four years younger than her, single, and still living at home or on campus. After marrying Rod and reducing her class load to part-time, she'd become the older, nontraditional student. She felt isolated from the others. They would hang out at the campus cafeteria after class. She had to get home so Rod could take the Datsun to work.

It was a short walk to the parking lot. Darkness had settled over the campus, but it was warm for early May. A group of guys skateboarded along the sidewalk. Karen walked in the grass to avoid them.

The drive home was only about twenty minutes, a straight shot from YSU to their trailer park in Frizzleberg. She hummed along to "Go Your Own Way" by Fleetwood Mac, "It Feels like the First Time" by Foreigner. She liked the new music but was still a Beatles fan. Nothing could top "Hey Jude" or "Yellow Brick Road."

It had been Rod's idea to rent a trailer halfway between Youngstown and New Castle. Since her parents had helped him get a job at the Rockwell Spring Division, he could work afternoon or midnight shift, and they wouldn't have to buy another car. Karen could finish school, and they would save enough money to build a house. It sounded like a good idea at the time, but here she was four years later, still commuting to school.

Karen followed the looping street and parked beside their trailer. It wasn't fancy, but the cream-colored siding and green trim were in good condition. She lugged her backpack up the steps. The door was unlocked. Rod was napping on the couch with feet propped over the arm. *The Rockford Files* blared on TV.

"Hey," Karen said. "I'm home."

Rod opened his eyes and yawned. "I guess I fell asleep. What time is it?"

Karen dropped her backpack on the floor. "About 9:30."

"It's early then." He sat up. "I saved you some pizza."

"Thanks," she said. "I'm starving."

"How was class?"

"Okay," she said. "I'll be glad when this quarter's over." She peered into the fridge and slid the pizza box out. Two pieces of pepperoni. That would do.

"Do you have a lot of homework for the weekend, or do we have time for a movie Saturday?"

Karen sat in the living room chair with the pizza box on her lap. She chewed cold pizza and swallowed. "I've got a book to start, but nothing for art history. What's playing?"

Rod reached for the paper on the end table and flipped through the pages. "*The House by The Lake* is at the Hi-Lander."

"Isn't that a scary one?"

"Yeah. *Fun with Dick and Jane* is at the Skyline and *The Enforcer* with Clint Eastwood is at the Super 8."

"I suppose you want to see Clint Eastwood."

Rod looked up from the paper and grinned.

"Let's go to that one," Karen said between chews.

After finishing the pizza, Karen emptied her backpack and spread her homework out on the kitchen table. Rod wandered back to the bedroom and dressed for work. Some new cop show droned on the TV. Before she knew it, it was time for Rod to leave.

"I'm off." He gave her a peck on the lips. "See you in the morning." He exited into the dimly lit yard. It was relatively quiet for a Friday night in the trailer park, but it was still early. The bars wouldn't close until two.

It was easier to share the car when Rod worked midnights instead of afternoons, but Karen hated it. The trailer park seemed safe enough, but she didn't know any of the neighbors very well. If someone wanted to break in, the trailer's flimsy door wasn't going to keep them out. All it took was an argument down the street or a strange bump in the night to wake her. Maybe she'd taken too many criminal justice classes before switching to sociology, but she couldn't help but imagine the park was full of unseemly people. She didn't get much sleep some nights.

Karen shuffled through the day's papers. She didn't feel like studying. The *Life after Life* book sat on the back corner of the table. Dr. Greenman said it was a fast read. Maybe it would be boring enough to put her to sleep. She grabbed an iced tea from the fridge and cuddled up on the couch to read.

Foreword. She skipped that. *Introduction.* "This book, written as it is by a human being, naturally reflects the background, opinions, and prejudices of its author." Blah. Blah. Blah. He wasn't giving a firsthand account. He didn't know anything about occult phenomena. He was a Presbyterian. Okay. PhD. Blah. Blah. Blah.

Karen sipped the iced tea. So far, it wasn't very interesting. Chapter 1. The Phenomenon of Death. "The subject of death is taboo." That was certainly the truth. Her mother was a professional at avoiding the entire subject. People passed. They didn't die. Blah. Blah. Blah. "During the past few years, I have encountered a large number of persons who were involved in what I shall call 'near-death experiences.'"

Hair raised on the back of Karen's neck as she read his list of three categories. There were people resuscitated after being declared clinically dead, those in accidents who came close to death, and secondhand accounts.

Chapter 2. The Experience of Dying. "A man is dying and, as he reaches a point of greatest physical distress, he hears himself pronounced dead by his doctor. He begins to hear an uncomfortable noise, a loud ringing or buzzing, and at the same time feels himself moving very rapidly through a long dark tunnel."

"Oh, my God," Karen whispered. She read the sentence again.

What kind of book was this? She checked the cover. The author was Dr. Raymond Moody. A doctor. He had a PhD in philosophy from the University of Virginia and a PhD in psychology from the University of West Georgia. And an MD the previous year from the Medical College of Georgia. The man certainly had an education, and he was conducting research.

"A long dark tunnel." After all these years, Karen had convinced herself that her memory of the tunnel was her imagination. She was never pronounced dead, was she? Mom had brushed off Karen's recollection like she did everything else. Karen figured it was just some childhood dream. Maybe a side-effect from the anesthesia she'd been given at the hospital when she had her tonsil surgery.

She read carefully through each chapter. Some people heard the doctors pronounce them dead or strange noises. She didn't remember any of that, but she did share the tunnel experience with others mentioned in the book. There was one man who had the experience as a little boy. He said the tunnel looked like a sewer. It didn't say if he was scared. That was one thing she did remember, the fear of losing Mom.

For a long time, Karen was afraid the dark tunnel would return and she wouldn't come back the next time. How many years had Mom lain in bed with her until she fell asleep? Is that why she was always drawing circular funnels? Is that why her wristwatches always died? For the first time in her life, she didn't feel like an alien. She wasn't the only one who'd experienced this sort of thing. *Near-Death Experience.* That was it. She wasn't crazy.

It was almost three in the morning when she finished the book. She went back and reread some of the sections. "The only person I tried to tell was my mother. Just a little later I mentioned to her how I had felt. But I was just a little boy, and she didn't pay any attention to me. So I never told anybody else," one person said.

Karen understood how he felt. Mom said she had been watching the surgery. She must have known. The more Karen thought about it, the angrier she got. She stayed up the entire night, reading through the experiences repeatedly.

By the time Rod returned from work, Karen had her mind made up. Before he could take off his boots, she grabbed her purse and headed for the door.

"Hey," he said. "What's going on? Where are you going?"

Karen waved the book in the air. "I have to talk to Mom."

"About what? She's probably not even out of bed yet."

Karen paused with her hand on the doorknob.

"What's going on?" he said.

She'd kept the story to herself for so many years, how could she possibly tell anyone now, especially Rod?

"Is it an emergency?"

"No," she said. "I just …" Could she just come out and tell him she'd had a near-death experience?

"Just what?"

After four years of marriage, Rod knew she wasn't a typical housewife. She liked strange paranormal stuff. She didn't enjoy cooking and cleaning. If that's the kind of woman he had wanted to marry, that certainly wasn't what he got. He seemed happy with her so far, but this was something else. "Tubular Bells" from the *Exorcist* movie echoed through her mind. This was more than looking for ghosts out in the cornfield. This was a mix of *Twilight Zone* and *Outer Limits*. How could she possibly explain?

"If you can't tell me, who can you tell?" he said.

"Yeah," she said. "I suppose I should explain."

She could barely get her lips to pronounce the words. *Near-Death Experience*. She started from the beginning and told him about her memory of the tunnel and the light at the hospital, how she'd asked Mom about it, but Mom had ignored her. Then she told him about the spirits in her bedroom when she was a kid, and the feelings she got when spirits were around.

"I didn't want you to think I was crazy," she said.

Rod chuckled. "Did you ever consider I might have married you because you are crazy?"

"This isn't a joke, Rod."

"I know that," he said. He reached his arms around her. "Hey, don't worry. It doesn't make a difference to me."

"I thought my memory was a dream." She felt relieved. "But this book is all about other people who have had the same experience as me."

"Well," he said, "then you're not crazy."

"I still have to go see Mom." She backed out of his embrace. "She was right there watching the surgery. I can't believe she wouldn't tell me what happened. I asked her directly too."

Rod sat down and unlaced his boots. "Don't be too hard on her," he said. "Try to see it from her point of view."

"That's easy for you to say," she said. "You haven't been living with this your whole life. She has some explaining to do."

Karen didn't know what she expected Mom to say, but she wasn't surprised by her reaction. Yes, Karen had died on the operating table. No, she didn't want to talk about it. That was in the past. It wouldn't do any good to discuss it. It was time to move on.

CHAPTER 16

AUGUST 1912: LILY DALE

Train breaks hissed. Lydia was shaken from sleep. Metal creaked. She opened her eyes. A great cloud of smoke and steam billowed past the window. Annie sat across from her staring out the window, forehead bumping against the glass. To their left, a smooth lake stretched to a tree-lined shore. Lydia had heard that Lily Dale was a small village. Amid the trees stood wood-frame buildings, but from this distance it was difficult to distinguish one from the other.

After living in the city, it would be refreshing to be away from the crowds and noise and the unrelenting smoke. She looked forward to ignoring all the newspaper reports. First was the sinking of the Titanic in April. Everyone was still talking about it, including Edward. How did it sink? What went wrong? Did they not see the iceberg coming? Why were there not enough lifeboats?

Now they were in the middle of a ruthless presidential campaign. In March, Teddy Roosevelt said if Republicans didn't nominate him, he would run as an independent. William Taft won the Republican nomination, but Roosevelt didn't want to accept the decision. He broke with tradition and showed up at the convention. When he wasn't nominated, Roosevelt announced he was forming a new party. It was such a mess, Lydia vowed to stay out of politics for the rest of her life. Edward told her she was being silly. That was the way politics worked.

"The lake is beautiful," Annie said. "Nothing like watching

the ocean from Glamorgan, but beautiful just the same."

Lydia slid Alice Stansfield's letter from her purse, unfolded it, and read the directions. "Alice said we should go to the Leolyn Hotel. It's across the bridge from the station." It was still hard to believe that William and Alice had moved to Rochester. She couldn't blame Alice for wanting to live near her son, especially now that William suffered from a heart condition. Lydia was first to admit that she didn't have the strength to keep up the good fight without them, especially with the asthma taking its toll. Annie's support was essential, but with a baby girl just six months of age to care for, she didn't have much time to devote to the fight either.

"There's the bridge." Annie pointed to the white wooden structure.

The train glided into the station. Lydia joined her at the window. The stop wasn't a station. It was a covered platform with gray painted floorboards. A dozen or more people, mostly women, waited with luggage. Two boys stood by with hand carts ready.

Once the train stopped, the passenger car came to life. Three women from Pittsburgh whom they'd met earlier in the day, spent no time getting their bags and moving toward the exit. An elderly gentleman who had spent the trip reading, remained in his seat. Maybe out of courtesy, he let the women go first. Or maybe he just wanted to avoid the initial rush. Besides a nod of greeting, he hadn't said a word for hours. The other seats were occupied by a group of older women who had gotten on near Erie. Alice said that weekdays were slower than weekends, but this Thursday seemed busy already.

Annie stood, smoothed her gray skirt, and grabbed her suitcase from the overhead. "This will be an exciting stay," she said. "Let's make the best of our time."

Lydia rose from her seat. Her left leg was stiff from the journey but would soon loosen up with a little walking. She slid her valise from the overhead, forgetting how heavy it was. Her bag was twice the size as Annie's. She'd probably brought too much for a four-day stay, but her mother always taught her to be prepared. Three pairs of shoes might be necessary if it rained.

One always needed an extra coat for cool evenings.

"I told you not to bring the kitchen sink." Annie grinned.

"Thank goodness there are porters," Lydia said. She couldn't imagine carrying the bag all the way to the bridge.

A short boy with a black leather cap and gray plaid vest took no time in greeting them as they stepped from the train car. "Help you to your hotel?" he asked.

"Yes, please," Lydia said.

"How much?" Annie asked.

"Five cents," he said.

"That's highway robbery," Annie said. "I'll carry my own."

"I can do both bags for six," he said.

"That's better," Annie said.

"You staying at the Leolyn or someplace else?"

"My friend, Mrs. Marquette, will pay you when we reach the Leolyn Hotel."

The boy loaded the bags on his cart and rushed ahead of them.

The Leolyn Inn was surrounded by a big front porch overlooking the lake. The lobby was small, but impeccably clean. Lydia was impressed. When Alice said Lily Dale was a camp, she had imagined more rugged accommodations. Maybe a log cabin with a fireplace. Instead, the place was filled with the sweet odors of fresh roses.

An older woman greeted them at the desk. The porter had already taken the bags to their room and the hostess had a key ready for them. Lydia was impressed that the lad had caught her name and checked their room reservation. She gave him a one-cent tip when they reached the room.

The window had been opened and pine-scented breezes softly stirred the curtains. Songbirds tweeted happily. The twin beds had matching floral covers and plush pillows. A side table held an ornate lamp with beaded shade. There looked to be no electricity in the building. Beside the lamp was a tin of matches to light the wick.

Annie ignored her bag and gazed out the window. She paced back to the bed and perused an event flyer that had been left on the side table, but she didn't stay seated for long.

Lydia unpacked her dresses and hung them in the wardrobe before they became too wrinkled to wear. She thought she should rest after the long trip, but she didn't feel tired. Just the opposite. The energy here was striking. It was as though the curtain between the spirit world and the physical plane hung thin like gauze here. She wouldn't even need Charley's help to reach the other side. It was a mere step away.

Annie stretched her lower back. "Leave that for now," she said. "Time's a wasting. There are so many things to do and see."

"I suppose you're right," Lydia said.

"Let's find Alice."

Lydia nodded. Annie locked the door and slid the key into her purse. Across the road a colorful garden was in full bloom. They walked the length of the dirt driveway careful to avoid the horse droppings.

"There's the entrance gate," Annie said. "Where's Alice staying?"

"South Street." Lydia pulled the letter from her purse. "I'll check the number."

Annie grumbled about the twenty-five cents per day admission fee, but grudgingly paid it. They strolled past the post office and a few other buildings, surprised to find South Street was only a stone's throw from the gate. A few people were out on the streets, but the village was welcomingly quiet. They quickly found the small wood-frame home, painted white and trimmed in blue and green. A wood placard, sticking up out of an herb garden in the front yard said, Spiritualist Medium, Readings 5 cents. Annie climbed the steps, knocked on the screen door, and fidgeted with the tassels of her purse.

Alice opened the door and stepped out onto the porch already wearing her hat. "You are just in time," she said. "There's a reading at Inspiration Stump in ten minutes."

"Inspiration Stump?" Lydia asked.

She descended the steps to the street. "Come. We want to get a good seat."

Lydia was surprised. She thought they would at least be invited in for a cold glass of iced tea after their long journey.

Alice was normally an excellent hostess. Maybe that was the way things were here at Lily Dale. They'd sponsored women's suffrage events the last few years. Susan B. Anthony had even spoken here. Lydia supposed freedom meant more than the right to vote. It meant freedom from expected drudgery and freedom to pursue one's own interests. That she could appreciate.

"How was your trip?" Alice asked. "I hope your room at the Leolyn is satisfactory."

"Oh, yes," Annie said. "But I don't expect to be spending much time in the room."

"I can understand that," Alice said. She led them to the top of the street. They turned right and followed a group of women, soon reaching a grassy path leading into a wood. At first, it seemed like a normal forest path, but as they went deeper the trees grew taller and straighter. Lydia felt odd. It was as if she had entered a room; no, a church or cathedral. It felt enclosed, but there was no roof and there were no walls. It was as if they were covered by a large glass dome.

Annie chuckled. "If I didn't know better, I would guess this is a place for the Tylwyth Teg."

"The what?" Lydia asked.

"Fairies," Annie said.

"You might spot a fairy or two if you're paying attention," Alice said. "The veil is so thin you can almost walk into the spirit world."

They reached an open area with plank benches. At least a hundred people were already seated. Lydia looked back. Others were following. She couldn't believe all these people were tucked into this quiet village.

Alice found empty benches in the third row from the front. "Sit here," she said.

Lydia gathered her skirts and sat next to a gentleman with a white handlebar mustache who smelled of pipe tobacco. Annie moved in beside her. Ahead there was no stage or lectern, only the stump of a tree large enough for four or five men to stand on. It must have been hundreds of years old when it was cut.

"I don't understand the meaning of the stump," Annie said.

Lydia shrugged. "Maybe it has no meaning," she said. "But you can't deny that this is a special place."

Four women and a man strolled to the front of the audience. A middle-aged stout woman mounted wooden steps to the top of the stump.

"Welcome to Inspiration Stump," she said. "For those of you who have not been here before, we will have three mediums give readings today. I ask that if you are called, you stand so the medium can communicate with you better. Please answer any questions directly, and loudly so you can be heard."

A few more people slid into seats and the crowd quieted.

The woman introduced the first medium as one of the members of Lily Dale. She brought four spirits forth for people before ending her demonstration. The woman gave many details as well as comforting an audience member who was obviously grieving for her father who had passed earlier that year. Lydia was impressed.

The man who stepped up on the stump next looked familiar to Lydia. She didn't think it was someone she'd met, but he reminded her of someone she couldn't place. His first reading was for a woman sitting at the back of the crowd. He brought messages and confirmation from the woman's grandmother and great-aunt.

"I have a small baby girl," he said, pointing in their direction. She thought he was directing his attention to a person behind them. "No, not one. Two."

Annie raised her hand.

"Two small girls," he said. "They have passed to the other side."

"Yes," Annie said.

Lydia was shocked. Annie had never mentioned losing any children.

"They passed, one after the other."

"Yes," she said.

"Cassie and May."

"Cassie and Elsie May." Annie's eyes rimmed with tears.

"Your mother says they are with her. She is keeping them

safe." The man breathed deeply. "And you have the gift also. Are you a medium?"

"Yes," Annie said.

"Ah," he said. "Now I understand. Your mother says you must rely on friends if you are to be successful."

Lydia took Annie's hand in her own. "We are here for you." Annie nodded.

"Do you understand?" he asked.

"Yes," she said. "Yes, I do."

After the demonstration, Alice joined them on the path. "You never mentioned the loss of your girls."

Annie wiped her eyes. "Cassie was taken by meningitis," she said. "Elsie from cholera. It was a sad time."

CHAPTER 17

AUGUST 1912: WOMAN'S DAY

Lydia rested in the quiet hotel room with a damp wash cloth covering her face. Asthma attacks always came at the most inopportune times. Thank goodness, Alice had brought along all her potions and concoctions. They did work to control the attack, but they didn't stop the fear that another might follow. Lydia didn't want to miss any of the day's activities, but she'd promised herself she'd rest for an hour.

There was a light knock at the door. It swung open on squeaky hinges. "Lydia?" Annie said. "Are you awake?"

"Yes." Lydia breathed through the damp cloth. Her lungs seemed to be working normally.

"The suffragettes are speaking at the auditorium in a few minutes," Annie said. "I didn't think you'd want to miss."

Lydia sat up in the bed and patted her hair. "I must look a mess," she said. She stood and smoothed out the wrinkles in her skirt.

"Nothing a bit of combing won't fix." Annie tossed Lydia's flowered hat on the bed. "Come on. Alice is waiting for us."

Lydia glanced at the dresser mirror. Her hair was a bit flat on one side, but it would have to do. She cocked her hat to the side to hide the problem.

"Here's your gloves and purse." Annie grabbed her by the hand and whisked her from the room.

The auditorium was almost full when they arrived. Alice waited near the middle.

"There are three seats together," Alice said. "Near the back." Gertrude Nelson Andrews was welcomed as the first speaker. The pale and graying, middle-class woman was born in Ohio where she had married a hotelier but eventually moved to New York. She authored several plays, belonged to the National American Woman Suffrage Association, and spoke at local clubs about civics, sociology, and other subjects related to the suffrage movement. Lydia hoped that when she was in her fifties, she had half the energy that Mrs. Andrews had. It would be nice to be a world changer.

Harriot Stanton Blatch followed. Lydia was surprised to hear she'd graduated from Vassar College with a degree in mathematics. She'd lived in Germany after college and married an English brewery manager. She'd even worked with Susan B. Anthony on the book, *History of Woman Suffrage*. After returning to the United States in 1902, she reinvigorated the American movement and organized and led the New York suffrage parade just two years before.

"You see," Alice said. "You can't let anything hold you back."

Lydia had to admit, the women were inspiring, but she wasn't sure she had the leadership ability or the good health to build a church.

After the speakers finished, Alice invited them to attend another gathering at a private home. Lydia's lungs had recovered, and she was happy to comply. They walked along the main street, passing a house with a single turret and another with an ornate front porch and upper balcony.

"This is it," Alice said. She grasped Lydia by the elbow and guided her up the porch steps to the double entrance door of the white house. They entered without knocking. Over a dozen people had gathered in the parlor.

Lydia recognized Effie McAffee, who'd given a talk the previous day on Scandinavian literature. She had been introduced as a distinguished woman and supporter of woman's suffrage movement. Lydia thought her talk was highly informative. Toward the back of the room, Bruce Calvert held a group of people in discussion like a king holding court. The balding gentleman with wire-frame glasses was from Indiana, but his beliefs were quite strange and eclectic for a midwesterner. He had formed a group trying to eliminate Christmas shopping, and someone said he was a nudist. She wasn't familiar with his publication, *The Open Road*, but he was said to be an anarchist and free-thinker. She couldn't imagine what trouble he would start if he lived in New Castle.

Mr. Richardson stood a head taller than everyone else, near the fireplace with a half-full glass of water watching the room. Alice had pointed him out the previous day. He was president of the Lily Dale Association.

Alice pushed into the room, greeted several people, and introduced Annie and Lydia. She stopped near an older woman and a well-dressed man with short, cropped hair graying at the temples and shaved face.

"Amelia," Alice said, "I'd like to introduce you to two friends from New Castle."

Amelia, Lydia discovered, was the hostess. The man was Reverend Frederick Wiggin.

"Pleased to meet you," Reverend Wiggin said with a soothing smile.

Lydia felt as if she'd been submerged in water. Charley was nearby but wouldn't approach. There were other spirits here too. Everything was disorienting, like the room was about to turn on its side. She wondered how the others could carry on a conversation.

"I think everyone is here," Amelia said. "Shall we get started?"

She led them to the dining room. The table had been pushed to the side and hardbacked chairs arranged in a circle. Lydia followed Alice's lead and sat near the front window. The day had been hot, but a cool breeze blew off the lake, rustling the lace curtains. Lydia breathed deeply. Her head began to clear.

"I think I know most of you here," Amelia said, "so, I will forego the introduction. We are pleased that Reverend Wiggin is able to grace us with his presence this evening. As you know, the reverend is a trance medium. Tonight, we will have the honor of speaking with his spirit guide."

Reverend Wiggin thanked everyone for coming. "First, let me explain," he said. "The order in which possession is taken is always the same. The period during which the taking of control is affected is several minutes before Mr. McCullough begins to speak. So, I ask for your patience."

Reverend Wiggin sat back in his chair and closed his eyes. A perceptible stillness came over the room. Even the curtains settled. The reverend's eyes remained closed. Except for an occasional spasmodic movement or an eye flutter, he looked to be sleeping.

Just as Lydia thought she might fall asleep herself, John McCullough emerged.

"Good evening, friends." He spoke slowly and methodically. "In the human life, there are mind states existing, which are analogous to the fog states, the rain, the intense dense moisture of the physical world, which shuts out the rays of sunlight. It is not for your body to lift these fog states, these mind attitudes. It is for your soul to do that, rather you, as a soul."

Lydia remembered the feeling of being submerged when she entered the house.

"I have been able to build up an aura to surround you. You are now in that aura. You are feeling it now. You cannot see it because you have not clear vision. When the soul expresses itself, there is always clear vision. Clear vision beholds the thing."

Lydia's mind wandered a bit as Mr. McCullough spoke through the reverend in his ponderous style. Effie sat in a meditative pose directly across from her. Annie's hands lay palm up on her lap. Her breathing was shallow, and her eyes closed. Alice nodded off, but most of the group sat in rapt attention.

"Health is a very tangible something, because it is soul. The soul must fail of fully expressing itself where ill health, or disease, expresses itself in any measure. Ill health is one of the fogs and damps," McCullough said. "Sickness is a negation. Your soul is able to raise you out of this negative state. You will be raised from this negative state this evening."

Lydia touched her throat. She felt that the spirit guide was talking directly to her. Was her asthma a negative state? Is that what was wrong? She never thought that she could rise above it in a spiritual way. Maybe she had been looking at things the wrong way.

"The soul is not stirred by noise and clamor. The soul seeks health and happiness."

Reverend Wiggin shifted slightly in his chair. "I have Esther's mother with me now," he said.

"That's me," a young woman with sad brown eyes said.

"The mother assures me that the bond between you continues," he said. "You have recently found a brooch in a drawer or box."

"Yes," Esther said.

"The mother said this was a sign to you. She is always with you."

She pulled a hanky from her purse and blotted her eyes.

"This is not a time for sadness," the spirit said.

"I know." Esther sat upright. "I know."

"That is all for now."

"Thank you," Esther said.

"Anna. Annie. Agnes," the spirit said.

"That's me," Annie said. "Annie."

"And the daughter," the spirit said.

"Yes," she said. "Agnes is my daughter."

"These talents must be developed. The auras can be sensed. The spirits can be identified. Do not put off these abilities. They must be nurtured like a small shoot. The leaves must develop. The flowers must bloom."

"I understand," Annie said.

"That is all for now."

"Thank you."

"The one who cannot breathe," the spirit said.

Lydia glanced around the room. Did he mean her? No one else responded.

"Yes," she said.

"We have pressure from disagreeing properties for digestion," the spirit said. "The circulation is drawn to other portions of the body which produces spasmodic asthmatic conditions of the bronchi. This makes for a filling of the tubes and a shortening of the breath and slowing of the circulation through the lower lungs." He followed with a list of oils including eucalyptus that should be added to pure grain alcohol and vaporized.

"That is all."

"Thank you." Lydia searched through her purse. She found Alice's letter folded inside and a stubby pencil. She quickly wrote down the list of oils before she forgot.

The readings continued for an hour or more. Lydia was exhausted but exhilarated by the end. It felt strange to be in a town that accepted spiritual readings as a normal daily event. There was no worry that some minister was determined to have you jailed, or that people looked at you strangely at the market. If readings were this accepted in New Castle, she and Annie could easily form a church. But that was wishful thinking.

CHAPTER 18

SUMMER 1981: ROAD TRIP WITH MARILYN

Karen finished her degree, and the house she and Rod had saved for was completed in 1979. She settled into a normal life and there was no further discussion of her near-death experience with anyone. When psychics like Jeane Dixon, Sylvia Browne, or Uri Geller appeared on TV, she didn't mention them.

They hadn't been blessed with any kids yet, but knowing how much trouble Mom had had, Karen decided she would be just as happy with a good career. She applied for jobs and decided to try volunteer work in the interim. In December, she spotted an article in the newspaper about the task force on domestic violence. They were looking for volunteers to work the phones at the crisis shelter. Karen called, and was soon working at their undisclosed location. It was nothing fancy, just an office with a desk and two phones, and a meeting room in the back. Karen worked whenever they needed her, usually alone.

She first noticed Marilyn Fair at group meetings and other occasions. Marilyn was about Karen's height, thin, with shoulder-length dark hair. She was quiet, so Karen didn't get to know her until one day when the conversation turned to art, and she discovered Marilyn was an artist. Karen eventually visited Marilyn at her dad's house and was impressed with her artwork.

"Have you ever tried using an airbrush?" Karen asked.

"No," Marilyn said. "I just work with pencil and paints."

"You could make good money at the fairs," Karen said.

"I don't know about that," Marilyn said. "Besides, I'd have to learn how to use one."

"I know someone who can teach you."

Karen introduced her to Larry at the fair that summer. It wasn't long before Marilyn had established her own business. She painted t-shirts, portraits, and landscapes, and did custom jobs on cars, vans, and motorcycle tanks. She designed a *Back to the '50s* logo for the new local car event and painted it on Chuck Lombardo's garage door. Her crowning achievement was a fantasy landscape that she painted on the side of her van. A wizard stretched his arms as he cast a spell against a darkening blue sky. His long white beard swirled across the painting. Gargoyles crouched at his feet.

Karen and Marilyn became fast friends. Marilyn was the sister she never had. Eventually, Karen found a position at the welfare department. Marilyn worked at the post office, but they continued to travel to car shows together during the summer. Karen always thought once she graduated, she'd leave the county fairs and car shows behind. She must have had some of Dad's fair-blood in her. She guessed it was all the activity that attracted her.

Their second trip to the Dover, Ohio, car show started like any other weekend. They loaded up the van with all Marilyn's art supplies and hit the road. Dover was about a two-hour ride from New Castle. Karen looked forward to seeing some of the usual gang. Stumpy, a big man with bib overalls and red hair, was happy to hear Marilyn was returning to paint cars on t-shirts. Her work had been popular the year before.

Dover was built on a flat plain and spread out in all directions east of the interstate. Unlike New Castle, most of the homes were little square boxes that all looked the same. They followed a four-lane highway into town and stopped at a gas station. Marilyn filled the tank and Karen got out to stretch her legs. A woman in the next car stared at the design on the side of the van. Karen figured she was admiring the artwork.

"Hi," Karen said, always ready to promote Marilyn's work.

"What's that on your van?" the woman asked.

"A fantasy painting."

"That's from the devil," the woman said.

"It's a wizard," Karen said. "It's make-believe."

"Oh, no," the woman said. "That's the devil's doing, all right."

Karen started to open her mouth and set the woman straight, but Marilyn's timing was impeccable. She peered around the back of the van. "Come on, Karen. Let's go."

The woman rolled up her car window.

"What was that all about?" Marilyn asked as Karen climbed up onto the seat.

"That lady thinks we're into devil worship or something." Karen frowned. If the woman knew about Karen's experiences, she would be even more aghast. "It's no use talking to some people."

Marilyn glanced in her rearview mirror. "Yeah," she said. "You have to be careful in some of these little towns." She started the engine and "Another Brick in the Wall" by Pink Floyd blared on the radio.

"Let's get to the fairgrounds," Karen said.

They followed the street toward town. "We have a left turn up ahead," Karen said.

Marilyn pulled the van into the left lane.

Bam!

"What was that?" Karen said.

"Someone hit us." Marilyn put the van in park and glanced at the side-view mirror. "Oh, God. It's a little old lady."

Marilyn climbed from the van and rushed around the car to open the woman's door. Karen circled around the front. The left quarter panel was crumpled from the headlight to the door. The driver's door was also dented. It looked like it might not be drivable. The lady's headlight was broken, and the front dented in a bit, but it didn't look like much damage. She'd really made a mess of things.

"Are you all right?" Marilyn asked.

"Yes. Yes. I think so," she said. "I'm so sorry."

It didn't take long for the cops to show up. Two climbed

out of the cruiser and walked around the van. The older guy was slim, middle-aged with brown curly hair and glasses. He eyed the situation up and down like he was the Clint Eastwood character, Dirty Harry, and was looking for a fight. The younger guy followed his lead.

"Are you all right, ma'am?" Dirty Harry asked the woman. "What's happened here?"

"I don't know. I was trying to pass. Looks like I got myself into a fender bender," she said.

He took out a note pad and jotted a few notes. "You okay to drive?" he asked her.

"Oh yes," she said. "I'm fine."

"Okay. You sit still. I'll handle things from here."

Dirty Harry turned to Marilyn and frowned. "License and registration."

"Sure," she said. "They're in the van."

He put his hands on his hips and stared at the painting. Karen thought of the woman's comments at the gas station. Was this guy thinking the same thing? Or maybe he thought they were hippies and the van was full of drugs.

Marilyn returned with the documents and handed them to him. He looked them over.

"You from New Castle?" he said.

"Yes."

"What're you doing out here?"

"We're going to the car show," Marilyn said.

"Do you work?"

"Yes," Marilyn said. "At the post office."

"Post office, huh?"

Karen wondered if he thought she was lying. "And she's an artist," Karen added. "She makes good money selling t-shirts."

Dirty Harry turned to Karen. "And what's your name?"

"Karen Heasley," she said.

"And I suppose you're an artist too."

"No," Karen said. "I work for the welfare department."

"Yeah, right," he said.

"I do," she said. "Do you want to see my ID?"

He ignored her. Marilyn spent the next half hour explaining the accident.

"Changing lanes without caution," Dirty Harry said. "This will have to go through traffic court. We'll have the van towed."

"But it wasn't our fault," Marilyn said. "That woman ran into us from behind."

"I don't need no artists telling me how to do my job," he said.

"And what is your job?" Karen said.

Dirty Harry snarled.

"Let's just go," Marilyn said. She grabbed Karen's arm.

"In the car," the younger cop said.

Karen threw up her hands. She had taken enough criminal justice classes to know things weren't right. This was a simple fender bender. No one was hurt. It was something for the insurance companies to handle. If anyone should have been cited, it was the woman.

It didn't take long to get to the station, an old two-story brick building that had a City Hall sign on the front and Police sign on the side. They climbed out of the police cruiser and followed the cop inside.

"He's out to get us," Karen said as they entered the building.

"What are we supposed to do about it?"

"We have rights," Karen said.

"Well, don't get us into more trouble than we're already in."

A cop with short cropped blond hair at one of the desks glanced up at them as they entered the station. They followed Dirty Harry into a small office and sat across a desk from him. He shuffled through some papers and wrote down Marilyn's name and address on a form. "What did you say you are doing here in Ohio?" he asked.

"We're going to the antique car show at the fairgrounds," Marilyn said. "I'm an artist."

"We already told you that," Karen said.

"We're going to have to impound the vehicle," he said.

"Well, you're not going to find any drugs in there if that's what you're looking for," Karen said. She was mad now.

"You just stay in your seat, little girl."

She was no little girl. "We're entitled to due processes," Karen said. "I know my rights, and you'd better not find any drugs in that van."

"Shut up, Karen," Marilyn whispered.

Dirty Harry chuckled.

"Tell him you want to call your attorney."

The cop's smile soured. "That's not necessary."

"We get a phone call," Karen said.

"Okay. Okay." He turned the phone on his desk to face her.

"Do you know what you're doing?" Marilyn asked Karen.

"Trust me," Karen said. "You're entitled to legal counsel. Call Tom." He'd know what to do. This small-town cop wasn't going to take advantage of them.

"Okay," Marilyn said. She dialed the number and waited. After a short conversation, she turned to Karen. "Tom says not to agitate them, to plead no contest."

Karen nodded. It took another half hour to write up the paperwork on the report. Karen looked at her watch. It was after one. Marilyn was losing business for every minute they spent there. "Are we done now?" Karen asked.

"I guess we've got the rest of the day at the car show," Marilyn said.

Dirty Harry leaned forward on his desk. "That van's not in any condition to drive," he said.

Of course not, Karen thought. She couldn't tell if the damage had been enough to keep them off the road, but she was sure the cop would be ready to pull them over if they left with it.

"We'll get a ride home," Karen said.

"The welfare office is just down the street," the cop said. "Maybe they can find you a ride."

Karen's cheeks flushed. New Castle wasn't one of the most progressive places, but rural Ohio was worse.

"I'll call my dad," Marilyn said.

"We can call Rod's mom," Karen said. "I know she's home."

The rest of the day was a bust. They waited hours for Rod's mom to arrive. Then they had to have the van towed back to New Castle. In the end, Marilyn never got a fine from traffic court. It didn't look like they'd touched a thing in the van. Karen figured some spirits had been looking out for them. She didn't mention that to Marilyn.

CHAPTER 19

SEPTEMBER 1912: THE SEARCH

Annie fanned herself with the newspaper and walked the length of the empty meeting room. A church. It was just what she and Lydia were looking for, a room large enough to hold forty or fifty people for talks and special events, but cozy enough for weekly church services. A wall of windows, letting in what cool breeze there was on that hot August day, let in natural light. The ceiling was equipped with electric bulbs if they had evening meetings.

"This is perfect," Annie said.

Mr. Bolinger adjusted his suit vest over his protruding waist and twirled his mustache. Sweat ran along the side of his face. "There is a bath off the main hall," he said. "And we have folding chairs available for rental."

"We'll need to rent chairs, at least at the beginning," Lydia said.

"The beginning?" Mr. Bolinger glanced at Annie belly. "You are looking for a long-term rental?"

"Yes," Annie said. "We need a space for weekly church services and an occasional extra event."

"I see," Mr. Bolinger said. He steepled his fingers and pursed his lips. "And what sort of church will be meeting here?"

Annie's mouth soured. They had been excited about opening a church immediately after their stay at Lily Dale. Daniel had warned her that they might have problems renting a location, especially if a building owner remembered Lydia's trial. That was one reason Annie insisted they rent the room under Daniel's name.

"A Spiritualist church," Annie said.

"One of those Protestant denominations?" he asked.

Annie didn't want to answer. This was a free country, and he shouldn't have the right to ask. Freedom of religion. Lydia stared at her. Bolinger would find out eventually. They would need to advertise church services and who the visiting mediums were. There was no use hiding it from him.

"We're part of a new religion," Lydia said. "We're Spiritualists. We are starting the First Spiritualist Church in New Castle."

"Oh. Oh. I see." He smoothed back his greased hair and glanced about the room. "You said you need a weekly meeting location?"

"Yes," Lydia said.

"I don't think we can accommodate you," he said. "We have many people in need of meeting space. I don't think we can commit to a weekly meeting."

"Even on a Sunday?" Annie's cheeks warmed. She wanted to tell this man a thing or two, but she held her tongue.

Mr. Bolinger rung his hands and gave them a story about the cleaning woman needing to get the room ready.

"And if we were Methodists, would you be turning us away?" Annie said.

"I ..."

"Come on, Annie." Lydia took hold of her elbow. "Let's go. There are other places in the paper."

"If I were a man looking to hold some secret fellowship meeting here, I'm sure you'd have been signing the papers already," Annie said.

"I think you ladies should ..."

"That's right," Annie said. "We are ladies or we'd have more to say to you."

Lydia griped Annie's elbow harder and pulled her toward the doorway. "Thank you for your time, Mr. Bolinger."

"I have more of my mind left to give that man," Annie complained.

"That's what I'm afraid of," Lydia said. "I've been in jail.

The last thing I want is to have the police called. It would be all over the front page of the paper. And then you'd see how much cooperation we'd get in this city."

Annie led the way down the steps. When they reached the foot, Lydia pulled the newspaper from her bag and unfolded it. "There's a suite available at the bank," she said. "Let's look at that."

"As long as it's not any higher than the third floor," Annie said. "I've had enough steps for today."

Lydia laughed and opened the door for Annie. It was nearly noon, and Washington Street was bustling with traffic. Trolleys rumbled by, taking no heed of pedestrians crossing the street. Motorcars coughed and spit black smoke. Annie had seen two crashes in the last week, one involving a horse-drawn cart, the other an older woman with a hat decorated with stuffed birds. The woman survived, but the hat did not.

"We'd better find a place soon," Annie said. "It's too hot to be walking all over town."

"All these old Presbyterians and Methodists," Lydia said. "They're not going to change willingly. Even the Italian Catholics are having their share of problems, and there's no Christian religion any older."

"I know," Annie said. "The spirit world is so calm and accepting. There is so much light there. It's difficult to deal with the earthly plane sometimes."

Lydia stopped at the front door of the bank. "Let's look at one more."

"Fine."

A Miss DuShane met with them at the main desk and guided them up the stairs to the second floor of the National Bank of Lawrence County. The air was stifling in the stairwell. Annie followed, heels clicking on the stone steps. She was ready to go home and rest on the porch with a glass of lemonade.

"This is the suite." Miss DuShane opened the door, revealing an office divided into several rooms. "It has its own bath."

Lydia walked to the window. "It has a nice view," she said.

Annie peered into the smaller rooms. They needed a space to

hold church meetings. These rooms were too small. "This isn't the sort of space we need," she said.

"We have some other rooms. What is it you're looking for?"

"We need a meeting room," Annie said. "For a church."

Lydia cringed.

"Oh," Miss DuShane said. "I don't think we have anything available large enough for church gatherings. You might want to try McGoun Hall. I think they have meeting rooms."

"Thank you for showing us the place," Lydia said.

They followed Miss DuShane back to the main floor and wished her well. It wasn't much cooler outside. Soot and dust clung to the stagnant, humid air. The hiss and rattle of automobiles combined with the rumble of the steel furnace. Annie felt a headache coming on.

"McGoun's just up the street," Lydia said, adjusting her narrow-brimmed hat. "It won't hurt to give it a try."

Annie sighed. "Then I must get home," she said. "I'm feelin' tired."

New Castle Hardware sat next to the McGoun Hall. They had a display of Hanna's Lustro Finish in the front window along with other painting supplies. The sign said the finish could be used on all kinds of furniture and woodwork. Annie wouldn't invest in the floors of their house since they were renting but thought she would talk to Ross about refinishing the top of their kitchen table.

"This way in," Lydia said.

Annie didn't have the patience for another disappointment. If the spirit world was working to help them start a church, she certainly couldn't tell. It seemed to be one roadblock after the next. She took a deep breath and followed Lydia inside. The vestibule led to a wide stairway. Off to the right was a door with office written on the frosted glass window.

"It won't hurt to ask," Lydia said. She strolled to the door and turned the knob.

Inside the small office was home to two desks. A woman sat at one desk typing. The other desk was empty. The side window was open and there was a newfangled fan blowing air throughout the room. The breeze lifted Annie's hat from her head. She caught it before it fell to the floor.

"May I help you?" the woman asked.

"We've been looking for a hall to rent," Annie said. She felt her pulse throbbing at her temple.

"What size?" the woman asked.

"Forty or fifty people," Lydia said.

"And is this a meeting, a public talk? What sort of event?"

"Weekly church services," Annie said. "And an additional event now and then."

"Oh, I see," the woman said. She rose from the desk and retrieved a record book from the table near the window. "Let me see what we have." She leafed through the volume.

Annie peered at the pages but couldn't tell what the notations meant.

"It doesn't look like I have anything for you now," the woman said. "If you leave me your contact information, I might have something open soon."

"Of course," Annie said. She wrote down her name and number on a piece of paper. The woman clipped it to the file. "Thank you."

Lydia followed Annie down the steps. "Do you think she'll ever get back to us?"

Annie shrugged. "If not, we'll find another place."

"I so wanted to have our own place before Reverend Olds came to town," Lydia said when they reached the street. She placed a kerchief over her nose.

They waited for a horse-drawn wagon to pass and crossed East Street to Neshannock Avenue. Annie was glad Daniel agreed to move closer to town. She didn't have to take the trolley everywhere. When they reached Lydia's house, Lydia looked a bit pale.

"Are you feeling ill?" Annie asked.

"I'm fine," she said. "Just a little touch of the asthma."

"Now don't we make a pair?" Annie said. "I'll call Mary Fullmer when I get home. She said she could host a meeting. I'm sure she would be more than happy to entertain the Reverend Olds. It will be more comfortable in a home setting anyway."

"But it won't be a church."

"I know," Annie said. "But we'll have a church soon enough. You'll see."

The traffic thinned as Annie passed the Lutheran Church, but she was still careful to look both ways at the North Street crossing. More than once, she'd come close to being hit by someone in a motorcar. Their wood-frame, two-story house wasn't far from the intersection. She made her way around the west side to the back door. Agnes greeted her in the kitchen with little Violet nestled in the crook of her arm.

"See, Mama is home," she said. Violet stretched out a little hand.

Annie unpinned her hat and tossed it onto the kitchen table.

"Mrs. Evelyn said there was a call for you," Agnes said.

Annie rubbed her aching head. She was grateful that the landlady let them use her phone. Evelyn and Mrs. Ida, two widows sharing the front of the two-story house, were cranky most days and didn't like the children being too loud. Annie wished they could afford a telephone of their own, but Daniel's salary would never be enough, especially if they kept having babies. "Did she say who called?"

"She said something about the McGoun building," Agnes said. "They will have a third-floor room available in November."

CHAPTER 20

DECEMBER 1989: GIB TOWN AND BEYOND

Karen held Mom's hand while they sat by Dad's bed in the Jameson Hospital ICU. Rod stood near the doorway, arms crossed over his chest. A solitary heart monitor kept time with Dad's heartbeat. Beep. Beep. Beep. Dad drifted in and out of sleep.

"It was probably the cold air," Karen said. She'd been happy when they'd decided to stay at home instead of going to Florida. She liked Christmas up north. Florida people had their houses decorated with colored lights, but it didn't seem right without snow. It felt more like a theme park than a holiday display. Now she wished they'd gone south for the winter.

"It's not his lungs," Mom said. "It's his heart."

"He's going to be fine," Karen said. She couldn't believe he was seventy years old already. It seemed it was just yesterday when she and Rod got married. She had been employed as a social worker for almost twenty years. Where had the time gone?

Dad fidgeted. He'd insisted the nurses raise the head of the bed so he could see the nurses' station. That was just like him, not wanting to miss anything.

Karen remembered their last trip to Florida. She sat on the front porch of her parents' winter house, a double-wide trailer in St. Petersburg. She enjoyed the sunshine and lush greenery. No matter where you went in St. Pete, water was everywhere. Bays, estuaries, the Gulf. Seagulls squawked from morning until night.

Karen recognized the rumble of Dad's old silver Cadillac coming through the neighborhood. It wasn't long before the boat-sized car pulled into the drive.

Rod was first to get out. He stretched and rolled his eyes at her. Dad followed slowly. She'd never thought of him growing old, but the last year it had been noticeable. His face looked paler, his hair thinner. It was if he'd aged five years since September. The last trip to Disney World with Uncle Paul, he'd been spry enough to walk the length of the park. Now, he had trouble getting out of the car.

"How was Gib Town?" Karen asked.

"Good," Dad said. He struggled for breath as he climbed the steps. "Almost everybody was there. Even Stevie Lisko. You should have come along."

"Someone had to stay with Mom," she said. The last thing she wanted to do was visit Gib Town. Gibsontown was its real name, and it was a wintering spot for fair workers and carnie people around the country. Made up of a conglomeration of mobile homes, tents, and fair trucks, it gave the men a place to work on the rides during their down time. It was home to giants, hairy women, crab-handed people, and an assortment of entertainers. Dad was in his element there, but she'd had enough of the fair for her lifetime.

"Where's Mom?" Dad asked.

"Inside," Karen said. "Making potato salad."

Dad trundled inside. Rod slumped into a chair next to Karen. "Your dad's sounding out of breath all the time now," he said.

"I know," Karen said. "Mom says they're thinking about selling this place and coming back to New Castle."

"When did he retire? In '77?"

"Yeah," Karen said. He was only fifty-eight years old then, but he'd put in thirty-five years at Rockwell International. Rod wouldn't be so lucky. Both he and Mom lost their jobs when Rockwell closed in 1981. Rod had gone on to school to become an electronics technician. After working on radios for a while, he'd found a good job working on the state lottery machines.

"They haven't lived down here very long."

"Mom said Dad misses being at home," Karen said.

"I thought the cold was bad for his lungs."

"Yeah," Karen said. "But I'm not arguing with them."

* * *

It was about 6:00 pm when a woman brought a tray with a solitary bowl of Jello. Dad seemed weak, but he managed to feed himself.

"See," he said. "I'm fine. If they thought I was dying, they wouldn't have brought me something to eat."

Mom didn't look convinced.

"Why don't you go home?" he said. "I'm tired of everyone hanging around. Let me get some sleep and I'll see you in the morning."

It took an hour for Karen to convince Mom to leave. "Come over to our house," she said. "We'll eat and get some sleep. I'll bring you back early tomorrow morning."

At home, Karen warmed leftover wedding soup for dinner, but they didn't eat much. *Murder She Wrote* played on the TV. Karen put sheets on the guest bed and clean towels in the bathroom. Mom paced the length of the living room and stared out the window, watching fine flakes cover the front walk.

"Why don't you put your pajamas on, Mom?" Karen said. "It's almost nine o'clock."

"I'm okay," she said. "It's early."

Karen flipped through the TV channels. *Married with Children*, some movie that had already started, and a movie about Liberace were the only choices. She left it on Liberace. Maybe it would take Mom's mind off things.

Karen washed dishes and put the kettle on the stove to heat water for tea. Rod wandered into the kitchen. "Do you want me to call off work for tomorrow?" he asked.

"No," Karen said. "It's no use having all of us sitting in the hospital room."

"You sure?"

"Yeah," she said. "You go to bed. Get some sleep. I'll see you in the morning."

He kissed her on the cheek. "Wake me if you need anything."

"Okay."

The kettle whistled and Karen moved it off the hot burner. "Do you want some tea, Mom?"

"No," Mom said. "Not now."

Karen opened the box of Lipton on the counter and tossed a bag in a cup. She poured steamy water. Her glasses fogged. A feeling came over her like a warm ocean wave on the St. Pete beach. It hit her in the chest first. Her ears buzzed. Her breath caught as it passed through her. And then it was gone.

"Mom," she whispered. What was that? She shivered.

The phone rang. One. Two. Three rings.

"Are you going to get that?" Mom said.

Yes. Yes. She touched her chest. The feeling was gone.

"Karen?"

"Yes, Mom." She reached for the phone. "Hello."

"Hello," a woman said. "Is this Karen Heasley?"

"Yes," she muttered.

"This is Betty from the ICU," she said. "I'm sorry to tell you that your dad has passed."

* * *

Karen stood next to the coffin, between Mom and Marty McGonigle. Except for being a bit pale, Dad looked like himself. She was surprised by all the flowers, but Dad knew half the people in town. She should have expected as much. Visiting hours were scheduled from 2–4 pm and 7–9 pm at McGonigle Funeral Home. Nothing fancy. No funeral mumbo-jumbo. Just the way Dad would want it.

"If you need anything else, let me know," Marty said. He was the most recent in a long line of funeral directors. His family knew her family. Dad hadn't let Karen visit Obie before she died in the nursing home, but she remembered Obie's funeral here.

"Mary?" Father Daugherty strolled up the main aisle, black priest garb flowing beneath his coat. Mom's eyes filled with tears.

"I'll take care of this," Karen said. "Hi, Father."

"I came as soon as I heard."

"Thanks," Karen said.

"You have my sincerest sympathy," he said. He made the sign of the cross. "As you know, your father was not a regular at the church."

"I know," Karen said. Dad didn't have time for all the church dogma.

"I can't say a funeral mass for him," Daugherty continued.

Karen nodded. The last thing Dad would have wanted was a mass. He had made peace with the world long ago. "I understand."

"But I can say prayers."

"That'll be fine, Father," she said. "Thanks."

Father returned less than an hour later clad in white ceremonial robes. Karen sat with Mom while he said prayers and moved through the entire Rosary. It might not have been a mass, but Father said every prayer in the book. Maybe he thought Dad needed extra help. Not like he would be going to heaven according to the rules of the Catholic Church. Missing mass was a sin, and not a small one. Dad hadn't been given confession or last rites when he died.

Karen remembered the warmth that traveled through her before the phone call came from the hospital. Dad had passed, and if he hadn't gone to heaven, he had gone somewhere. She'd felt it. He'd seen the light at the end of the tunnel and didn't return. She didn't care what the Catholic Church had to say. He was in a good place.

Dad's brother, Paul, took a seat next to Karen. He was a taller, thinner version of Dad, with the same eyes and receding hairline. Now that Dad was gone, he was the only one of the boys left in the family.

"What's this?" he whispered.

"Prayers," Karen said.

"Your dad wouldn't like this."

"I know," she said. "What was I supposed to say."

By the time Father reached the end of his prayers, people were filtering into the room for calling hours. The next two hours were a blur of handshakes, I'm-sorrys, we-will-all-miss-hims, and tears.

Karen joined Paul outside for some fresh air. The snow had stopped but the wind had a nasty bite to it.

"How's your mom holding up?" Paul asked.

"Okay," Karen said. Mom was doing better than she expected and was determined to make it through the next set of calling hours.

"Your dad didn't need a priest."

"I know," Karen said. "Father Daugherty was there for the family. He means well."

"He'd think otherwise if he knew your dad."

Karen laughed.

"Your dad's okay," Paul said. "You know that, don't you?"

Karen glanced up at her uncle.

"I mean it," Paul said. "This might sound crazy, but I felt it when he passed." He looked up at the cloudy sky. "It was about 9:30. Honest to God. It felt like someone walked right through me."

Karen shivered.

"Obie would have understood," he said. "She had the sight. You know."

"I know," Karen said. "I felt the same thing."

* * *

Karen dreamed she stood in a field of beautiful flowers. The colors were so vibrant, they were like nothing she'd ever seen. And the sky—the sky was so blue it hurt her eyes to look at it. A young man on a palomino approached. His hair was dark and curly. He wore a brown leather WWII bomber jacket and rode with a gentle hand on the reins.

"Karen," he said.

She recognized his voice. "Dad?"

Dad had boarded horses on Pennsylvania Avenue when he was younger. He used to travel to New Mexico to break horses when he and Mom were first married. But he'd never been in

WWII. Scarlet fever had ruined his hearing and he couldn't enlist.

"It's you," she said, "What are you doing here?"

"I've come to say hello."

Karen laughed. Dad didn't need all of Father Daugherty's prayers. He was in heaven and he was happy.

CHAPTER 21

MARCH 1913: THE RAINS CAME

Monday night, Annie Johns woke from a fitful sleep to the sound of pounding. It was usually rainy and cold in March, but this year it had been raining for almost two days. Violet was cranky from teething and Raymond had a spring cold. If she could only get a full night's sleep, she would feel much better. But that didn't seem to be in the cards.

"What is that?" Daniel sat up in the bed.

Bang. Bang. Bang.

"I think the wind is blowing a tree against the house."

Bang. Bang.

Daniel climbed from bed and stumbled into the dark hall in his long johns. Boards squeaked beneath his feet as he made his way down the hall.

Bang. Bang. Bang.

Cold, damp air rushed into the house when the door opened. Annie heard another man's voice but couldn't hear what he was saying. It sounded urgent. She threw on a robe over her nightgown and peered around the corner. Lydia's husband, Edward, stood at the door with an upraised lantern.

"What's wrong?" she asked.

Daniel turned. "The creek's rising," he said. "Edward's invited us to go to their place."

"Now?"

"Lydia insisted," Edward said. "You know. Charley."

Annie felt a tingle along her spine. "Are we in danger? What about Mrs. Evelyn and Mrs. Ida?"

"Word is, the Neshannock is over its banks in Volant. It won't be long until it starts to rise here," Edward said. "Wake the ladies. They have a second floor. Tell them what's going on. If things get bad, we'll send help."

"Do you think it's going to be that deep?" They didn't own any new rugs or furniture, but what they did have would take hard-earned dollars to replace.

"Better safe than sorry," Daniel said.

Annie opened the door to the children's room.

"What's happening?" Agnes asked.

"Wake Mabel and get your clothes, coats, and boots on," Annie said. "Each of you pack a bag and bundle the little ones."

"It's the middle of the night."

"Do as I say."

"Yes, Momma."

It was nearly midnight when they left. Edward led the procession along Neshannock Avenue through the pouring rain. Daniel carried Raymond, Annie cuddled little Violet beneath her coat, and Agnes lugged several bags. Mabel tried to hold an umbrella over Annie's head, but it didn't do much good. Rain dripped down her collar and along her back.

Electric streetlights flickered. In the distance, the mills rumbled. Red light lit the cloudy sky. Most of the homes and buildings on Neshannock Avenue were dark. The river was a black void behind the houses across the street. Annie couldn't see if it was rising, but she'd seen it get as far as the front steps the previous year. The cellar had filled partly with water. She hoped Lydia and Charley were wrong, and the flooding would be minor.

Every room in the Marquette house was lit. Lydia greeted them at the front door.

"Come in out of the rain," she said. "We'll put the children up in the front bedroom. I have plenty of blankets."

Annie took off her coat and hat and hung them on the hall tree while the older girls followed Lydia up the steps with the babies, like a hen with chicks. Edward and Danny remained on the porch to watch the rain. Annie shivered and peered into the parlor. The rug had been removed from the floor and the upholstered sofa was stacked atop two end tables.

Lydia descended the steps to the entryway. "Would you like some tea?" she asked. "I have hot water on the stove."

"Sure." Annie followed her to the kitchen. The electric ceiling light buzzed. Lydia scooped loose tea leaves into a pot and added water from the kettle.

"Charley woke me at 10:30," Lydia said. "I had Edward call the railroad. You know. News travels fast along the rails. They said it's starting to flood across Indiana and Ohio. Railroad lines are shutting down in Dayton."

Annie sat at the kitchen table. "We've had floods before."

"Not like this." Lydia poured them each a cup of tea. Steam swirled into the cool air. "Charley is worried."

Annie thought of all the people sleeping in their homes along Neshannock Avenue. "Do you think we'll be safe here?"

"I hope so. We can go over to McGoun Hall if it gets too deep."

"I hope it doesn't get to that." Annie sipped her tea. Their Spiritualist church had come a long way in only half a year's time. Reverend Olds spoke before a small crowd at Mary Fullmer's house late in September last year. When he returned to New Castle two months later, he delivered his oration, "What Profits a Man by Spiritualism." McGoun Hall became home to both the First Spiritualist Church on Sunday under the direction of Youngstown medium Mrs. Ida Howard, and the Truth Seekers meetings on Wednesday, which were run by Mrs. Hattie Polonus, also of Youngstown.

They had been so successful that mass meetings were held in the Nixon Theater on a Sunday afternoon and evening in January. Prominent Spiritualists from Pittsburgh, Cashius L. Stevens, president of the Pennsylvania Spiritualist Association, and Reverend Arthur S. Howe, vice president and pastor of the First Church of Spiritualists, spoke to large crowds.

It was almost 2:00 am by the time Edward convinced Annie and Lydia to try to sleep. "We'll keep watch," he said. "If the water comes up, we'll let you know." Annie felt wide awake but decided to rest in the guest bed, still in her dress, rain boots near the door.

Annie didn't feel like she'd slept, but the next thing she knew, morning light filtered through the sheer draperies. She glanced at the clock on the bureau. It was after eight in the morning. She slid from the bed and looked out the window. Through the rain, she saw the side yard, the neighbor's front yard, and the street were under water. It was high enough to inundate the cellar but not high enough to reach the first floor. She felt relieved.

Lydia already had a breakfast of oatmeal, eggs, bacon, and toast ready for the rest of the family when Annie reached the kitchen. Violet sat in Mabel's lap, trying to eat cereal with a spoon. Raymond was focused on the bacon, something they couldn't afford to eat very often.

"Sorry, I slept in," Annie said.

"You needed the rest," Daniel said.

"And it looks like the flooding has slowed," Edward said.

"Good," Annie said. "We can go back to the house and check on the widows."

Lydia looked up from her plate, forehead creased in a frown. "It's not over," she whispered.

"That's not what I wanted to hear." Annie said.

After an hour of calm, the water began to rise again. From the front porch, they watched it rush down East Washington Street and swirl into Neshannock Avenue. When the mills went silent, Annie knew they were in trouble. Lydia pulled on her boots and waded to the neighbor's house. The elderly woman was not home.

"It's over my boots," Lydia said. "It'll be coming in the doors soon."

"We need to make a decision," Edward said. "Move upstairs or go."

Danny pointed toward town. "I see boats," he said. "We need to get the little ones out of here."

"Agnes and Mabel, get your things together," Annie said.

"I'll get a bag packed," Lydia said.

Water sloshed over the edge of the porch and into the entryway before they were able to flag down a fishing boat. Two men in overalls and short jackets brought the boat alongside the steps.

"What's happening?" Edward called out over the rain.

"The Diamond is completely underwater," one man said. "Three feet deep in some places. The Shenango is rising. The Seventh Ward is going under, and I heard Kilkenny is already swamped."

"We've got four children and two women that need to reach safe ground," Daniel said. "There are two elderly women up the street."

"And our husbands," Lydia added.

"They've opened the high school," the man said. "And some of the churches are taking in people. I can get you to the base of the North Hill on East Street. You'll have to walk up from there."

"That'll do," Edward said. "Ladies and children first."

It took two trips to get them all transported to the base of the hill. Annie went first with the children in tow. It was impossible to keep the little ones dry. By the time they entered the school, everyone shivered from the wet and the cold. Violet was a little wisp of a thing and Raymond was susceptible to all sorts of colds and fevers in normal times. Annie feared they would be overcome by sickness. She didn't think she could stand losing another child.

They were welcomed by a dozen women in the gymnasium. Annie didn't know if they were the Ladies' AID Society, the Red Cross, a church group, or just a bunch of women who had gathered together in a time of need. Whoever they were, they had blankets and dry clothing and food.

Once they recovered, Agnes, Mabel, and Lydia decided to join the volunteers. Edward and Daniel left with the rescuers. The electric failed during the day. As night fell, lanterns illuminated the room in gold tones. Violet and Raymond snuggled against Annie on a cot. As people poured into the building, the stories got worse. Railroad and streetcar service into the city had stopped, homes and businesses were under water, and hundreds of people were homeless in the cold weather.

Wednesday was no better. The covered Black Bridge broke free and floated downriver, smashing into a water intake house of the Carnegie Steel Company and then into the Franklin Railroad

Bridge. The Franklin Bridge, which had been weighted down with railroad cars filled with coal, collapsed that afternoon. The remnants of the Black Bridge then hit the old Gardner Avenue viaduct, taking it down by sunset. At the same time, the Grant Street Bridge broke apart and fell into the rushing water. The West Washington Street Bridge was the only one over the Shenango River still standing.

As they tried to make the best of their stay, the first news of casualties arrived. Police officer Tom Thomas drowned while attempting to rescue stranded people near the Shenango Tin Mill. A five-year-old boy accidently fell into the Neshannock Creek and was lost.

On Thursday, the waters continued to rise until afternoon. Daniel and Edward joined them for dinner. Already there was talk of food shortages. The water company was out of commission, so there was no tap water available.

"The Seventh Ward is gone," Daniel said. "Homes swept right off their foundations. Everything is under five feet of water." He didn't need to say the rest. If they had still been living there, they would have lost everything, maybe even their lives.

By Friday, the waters started receding. Police and National Guardsmen of Troop F were brought in to patrol the streets. The Marquettes and the Johnses returned with the other residents to their damaged homes. Lydia offered to keep the little ones.

The widows had survived the ordeal and hired a couple of mill workers to clean out the front of the house. Annie surveyed the mud and debris. It was worst in the kitchen where the water had pushed in the door.

"Nothing a little elbow grease can't fix," she said. For others, recovery wouldn't be so easy. Over one thousand homes had received water damage.

Edward waded down to the railroad station. Trains weren't running into New Castle yet. Too many tracks needed repairs. He returned home with word that Erie was sending a thousand loaves of bread to the city. The mayor asked for people in the county to donate food until the roads could be opened. Clean water was another matter. It would be another day or two until power was restored.

By Monday, shop owners had cleaned out their store fronts and assessed their losses, schools reopened, roadways and sidewalks were cleaned of debris, power and water service was restored. The city estimated that New Castle sustained $2 million in damages. Many people were homeless, but at least they hadn't been hit like Dayton, Ohio. Twenty feet of water had covered much of its downtown area, killing 123 people and displacing 70,000.

The following week, the First Spiritualist Church collected donations for those who had been devastated by the flood. Members were generous, even though most of them lived in the heavily damaged Seventh Ward.

By November, much of the city had recovered. Church meetings were well attended, the hall filled to overflowing. They had to secure additional seats. A second mass meeting took place in Youngstown that was well attended by the New Castle members.

In February 1914, the church sponsored a concert, with piano and song solos. Annie sat beside Agnes and Daniel in a chair near the front of the room. Mrs. Howard was joined by Mrs. Hunt and Reverend Mrs. Morrow of Pittsburgh, who gave an interesting talk on Spiritualism. Lydia, who had been elected president, presented Mrs. Howard with an emblem of Spiritualism to show their regard and love. She also assisted Ida on Sunday with tests and readings.

"You should be up there too," Daniel said.

"I know." Annie folded her hands in her lap. "I just have been so busy with the children."

"That's no excuse," he said. "You need to be ordained. We need a real church."

CHAPTER 22

2000: MOM'S GONE

Karen wiped her boots before opening the door to Mom's apartment. Marilyn followed her inside with two bags of groceries.

"Hi, Mom," Karen said. "We're back."

"Hi," Mom whispered.

Karen entered the living room. Mom sat propped up on the couch with a crossword puzzle book on her lap. The evening news played on the TV. Karen checked the oxygen line running from the tank and kissed Mom on the head. Bags rattled in the kitchen as Marilyn put away the groceries.

"How are you feeling?"

Mom shrugged. She didn't like being sick. She didn't like the prednisone the doctor had prescribed. When she'd first been diagnosed, she'd insisted she had "just a touch" of emphysema.

Karen still remembered the voice she'd heard that day. "This is what kills her," it said. She'd tried to forget the words, but that was becoming more and more difficult. When she'd first moved Mom into the apartment, she was only having problems climbing stairs. Now just walking to the kitchen was an effort. Not that Mom was giving in to her sickness. She still managed to fix her own lunch while Karen was at work.

"What'll it be for dinner?" Marilyn called from the kitchen. "We can do chicken or pasta."

"Whatever you want," Mom said.

Karen joined Marilyn in the kitchen. "Let's do pasta," she said. It had been a long day. "That will be faster."

Marilyn filled a pot with water and put it on the stove to heat. "Is Rod coming over to eat with us?"

"Not tonight," Karen said. She searched the refrigerator for vegetables to make a salad.

"What's that smell?" Marilyn said. "Is something on the stove burner?"

Karen removed a head of lettuce and green pepper from the crisper. "What smell?" She found cut-up onion in a plastic container.

"I don't know," Marilyn said. "It smells … um … like cigar smoke."

"Cigar?" Karen shut the refrigerator door and sniffed the air. "Yep. That's cigar smoke. Dad's here."

"Your dad?" Marilyn looked around the room. "What do you mean?"

"I've smelled it a couple of times before," Karen said.

"You mean a ghost?"

"No," Karen said. "Well, yes. Maybe like a ghost."

"What are you saying?"

Karen didn't want to go into the whole story about dying and seeing spirit people as a child. She and Marilyn might be as close as sisters, but as far as Marilyn knew, she was normal. She never told her about her dad's passing, the feelings she had when spirits were near, not even the apparition of a woman she saw crossing the road near Edwards Restaurant recently.

"When we bought this rental house, we cleaned everything," Karen said. "It even has a new furnace. I'm saying that smell isn't coming from the house. And it smells just like my dad's cigars."

"Oh." Marilyn raised an eyebrow. "I see."

"Let's just get the food ready," Karen said. "I'm starving."

* * *

Karen switched off the living room lamp. Mom's breath rattled. In. Out. In. Out.

"Stay with me," Mom said.

Karen squinted in the darkness. "Sure, Mom. Do you need

anything?"

"No," Mom said. "I don't want to be alone."

"Did you have another bad dream?" Karen took her hand. Mom had jumped off the couch after her last bad dream. She told Karen that she was being buried alive in a coffin. Karen felt bad for her. No matter how much she had tried to reassure Mom that the light was waiting for her, that death was nothing to be afraid of, she wouldn't listen.

"I just want …" Mom said, "… you with me."

Karen sat on the edge of the couch and took her hand. "I'll always be here for you, Mom."

Mom had taken care of her all those years growing up, now it was her turn to return the favor. She'd lost count of how many months she'd been living with her, neglecting her own home and husband. Dear Rod. He'd been a saint.

"I need to go," Mom whispered. "To the hospital."

"Are you sure?"

"Yes," she said. "I'm getting worse."

"I'll call Rod," Karen said. "We'll take you in the morning."

Karen packed a bag for Mom which included her robe and favorite slippers. When Rod arrived, he moved their Sebring convertible out of the way so they could take Mom's old white Plymouth.

After being admitted, Mom insisted Karen be given power of attorney.

"I don't think that's necessary," Karen said. "This is just a minor setback. The doctor will change your medicine like last time, and you'll back home in a couple of days."

Mom insisted, and they had an attorney bring in papers for Karen to sign. By the time he left, Karen's body ached. She never liked being in the hospital, and this time it seemed worse than usual. It was like she was absorbing everyone's sickness.

Mom adjusted the oxygen tube under her nose. "I don't know what to do about the funeral," she said. "I'm not Catholic like your dad."

"You don't need to worry about that now."

"Where are they going to bury me? I'm a Presbyterian."

"That's a long way off, Mom," Karen said.

"I don't want to be under the ground."

"We'll find a mausoleum, Mom," Karen said. "Let's not talk about this anymore. You need to focus on getting better."

As the day continued, Mom's skin paled. A doctor came in to check her, and there was talk of blood thinner to get rid of clots. Karen tried not to worry, but when a young nurse tried to insert a needle into Mom's arm with no success, Karen felt like the needle was jabbing her own arm.

"I'm so sorry," the nurse said. "I'm having trouble."

"Honey, go get a baby needle," Mom said. "My old veins are collapsing."

Collapsing, Karen thought. That couldn't be. Mom had been active her entire life, working part-time at Rockwell as a nurse, volunteering at the hospice, taking blood pressures at K-Mart, being the neighborhood nurse for all the kids. She'd decorated the apartment for Christmas just last month. She was always up on the news and current events. Her mind was too alert for her to be dying.

The next thing Karen knew, they were moving Mom to the Intensive Care Unit. She was attached to a heart monitor and IV bag.

"I should have quit smoking earlier," Mom said. "Now, I'm paying for it."

"How about this?" Karen said. "I'll check the TV guide and see if there are any good movies on next week. We can plan on watching. I'll even make popcorn."

Mom smiled, but her eyes were focused on a distant object. "Stay with me," she said. "I don't want to be alone."

"I'm right here, Mom."

Karen slumped in the brown leather chair and closed her eyes. The consistent beeping of the heart monitor lulled her to sleep.

"Karen," Mom said. "Karen."

Karen jumped up. "What is it?"

"I have to go to the bathroom."

"You can't do that," Karen said. "I'll call a nurse."

"I can do it myself." She slid her legs from the bed and stood.

"Mom."

"I can do it." She grabbed the IV pole and walked into the restroom.

Karen heard a crash. "Mom!"

Mom had collapsed and was struggling for breath.

"Help!" Karen called out.

An aide came to her rescue and carried her back to the bed. A nurse replaced the oxygen tube with a larger mask and scolded Karen for letting her mother get out of bed.

"You heard what the nurse said," Karen said. "No more getting out of bed. They'll bring a bedpan whenever you need it."

Mom mumbled something.

"What?"

Mom lifted the mask. "I don't want any resuscitation," Mom said. "I'm too weak. Something will break."

"Stop talking like that," Karen said.

"Tell the nurse," Mom said.

Karen sat on the side of the bed and held Mom in her arms. "Don't let them do anything," Karen heard Mom's voice in her head. I won't, Mom. We'll do things just the way you want them.

Mom stopped breathing. The heart monitor blared, and the nurse ran into the room. Karen shook her head. "She doesn't want resuscitation."

"Are you sure?"

Karen nodded. "Could you please leave us alone?"

Karen held the body in her arms. Where are you, Mom? she thought. Do you see it? Do you see the light? Is Dad there?

She closed her eyes, waiting to feel her spirit pass through her. Nothing. She didn't feel a tingle or a fluttering in her chest. There was no voice or smell. She was all alone. Mom was gone.

CHAPTER 23

2000: DEALING WITH THE GRIEF

Karen walked into the apartment and stood in partial darkness. A pillow, blanket, and oxygen tube still laid on the couch where Mom had slept for the last few months. She waited to hear Mom's raspy breath, but there was nothing. No breathing. No TV. Not even the sound of traffic in the distance. Dead. Everything was dead.

She shed her coat and sat on the couch, holding the pillow against her chest. She was an only child, raised to be independent and self-sufficient. Mom had worked hard to make sure she could take care of herself in any situation. Why did she feel so helpless and alone? Mom wouldn't want it that way.

Mom is gone.

Karen curled beneath the blanket, remembering the sound of the heart monitor going flat, Mom's last breath. Her own heart ached with loss. She sobbed into the pillow. Her confidant, her rock, her best friend was gone. She was an orphan.

She must have slept, because the next thing she knew, it was morning. She wandered into the kitchen. Mom's medicine bottles were lined neatly on the counter.

"A lot of good these did you." She gathered them up and marched to the bathroom. One by one she flushed them away.

"Damn it, Mom," she said. "I wasn't ready. Why did you have to leave so soon?"

She tossed the empty bottles into the trash.

The kitchen phone rang. Once. Twice. Three times. Four.

"Hello."

"Hi, Karen. It's Marty," he said. "I'm just calling to let you know we have your mom. I'm so sorry to see that she's passed."

"Thanks, Marty."

"I know this is a bad time," he said. "But if you want to bring some clothes down for her, we can make plans for the funeral."

"Sure, Marty," she said. "I'll be down later."

"Take your time," he said. "And if you need anything, just give me a call."

Karen hung up the phone and wandered into Mom's room. She opened the closet and stared at the clothes. They hadn't talked about what she would wear, or what kind of coffin she wanted. Nothing.

"Which one, Mom?" She ran her hand over dresses, blouses, and skirts. Green. That was a nice Irish color. Mom would like that. She removed a green skirt and flowered blouse and laid them on the bed. What else? The black shoes would have to do. And rings. Mom had taken off her wedding rings so she wouldn't lose them. Karen opened the top dresser drawer. The rings were gone.

The wedding bands had been sitting in that drawer for months. Mom had no reason to move them. Karen checked the other drawers, the kitchen, the living room.

"I can't find your rings, Mom."

A gentle warmth spread outward from her chest.

"Mom?" Karen's eyes filled with tears. "You're here."

The warmth traveled along her arms and legs.

"I know," Karen said. "The rings don't matter."

* * *

Karen stood by the coffin. Marty had done a good job with everything. Mom looked better than she had in weeks, her cheeks were pinker, and she seemed more at rest than she had in a long time. They'd selected a green coffin with the Irish blessing:

May the road rise up to meet you. May the wind be always at your back. May the sun shine warm upon your face; the rains fall soft upon your fields and until we meet again, may God hold you in the palm of His hand.

The calling hours were busy. Many of the nurses Mom worked with stopped in to give their condolences and say what a great nurse her mom had been. Other people knew her from when she worked at Rockwell. Then there were the women she socialized with.

Cousin Carol, daughter of Mom's sister, joined Karen at the coffin. "I'm so sorry this had to happen," she said. "We're all going to miss your mom."

"Thanks," Karen said.

"She looks wonderful." Carol kissed Mom on the forehead and touched her hand. "Where are her rings?"

"I don't know," Karen said. "I looked all over for them."

"They didn't get left at the hospital, did they?"

"No," Karen said. "She hasn't worn them for a while."

"That's strange."

"Yeah," Karen said. If they had been Dad's rings, she would have thought his spirit was playing a practical joke, but Mom was too serious for that.

* * *

Karen stared out the apartment's kitchen window, hoping Mom would touch her one more time, reassure her that everything was going to be okay.

"Are you ready to go?" Rod peered into the kitchen. "We need to be at the funeral home in ten minutes."

"Yeah," she said. Mom had passed on to the light. Karen knew it was real. Still, she couldn't shake off the grief. "Let me just check one more thing."

Karen entered the bedroom, hoping to see Mom standing there. The bedspread was smooth and untouched. Everything on the dresser was arranged just as Mom had left it.

Karen opened the top drawer. The rings were there, right where they were supposed to be. She touched them.

"What is it?" Rod asked.

"I couldn't find these rings for calling hours." She put the rings in her pocket. "Now they're here."

CHAPTER 24

MAY 2004: PSYCHIC FAIR

It had been almost four years since Mom died. Karen was still trying to come to terms with her passing. Her work in social services was rewarding, but she felt like she should be doing more with her life. If her near-death experience meant nothing, then why had she had it in the first place? Why had she seen spirits as a child? These weren't the types of questions she could bring up with Father Daugherty, but she attended mass every week, praying for an answer.

She needed someone to confide in besides Rod, someone to help her search for her purpose. She remembered the Caribbean cruise she'd taken with family and friends a couple of years before and the story Marilyn had told her.

Mini, one of her coworkers, was sharing a room with Marilyn. She had been seasick and Marilyn had been nursing her during the trip. One night, Marilyn woke during the night, sensing someone was in the room. At first, she thought someone had broken in, but she knew the door was locked. Moving against the faint light coming under the door, she saw a figure move toward her, then away. It looked like a woman in a nightgown, so she assumed Mini was trying to make her way around the bed.

"You can turn the light on," Marilyn said.

There was no reply. But the figure moved toward the door and into the bathroom. Still no light.

"Mini," Marilyn said. "I'm awake. You can turn the light on."

Still nothing.

Worried. Marilyn climbed from her own bed and turned on the light. Mini was still sleeping. She gathered the courage to check out the bathroom. When she turned that light on, there wasn't anyone there.

Marilyn recounted the story the next day and suggested telling the crew about the ghostly incident. Karen was still trying to avoid the truth about her own experiences. She insisted that they keep quiet about the incident, then she tried to forget it.

Karen didn't know if Marilyn's experience was a onetime event or if she had a special gift too. When she did bring up the subject, Marilyn wasn't surprised.

"You should have told me sooner," Marilyn said. "I just saw a poster the other day. There's a Psychic Fair in Warren, Ohio, next week. That would be a good place to start."

Karen was relieved and apprehensive at the same time. Parapsychology was one thing, but a *psychic fair* seemed more like fair gypsies and ride boys. She didn't want to be one of those "woo-woo" people. She wanted to have something respectable, like an education center.

On the day of the fair, Karen changed her mind five times before Marilyn arrived. No good Catholic would even consider a psychic fair. Half the people were probably faking and were there to take people's money. She wasn't that sort of person. What she'd seen was real. Spirits didn't belong at a fair.

When Marilyn pulled the car up to the house, Karen knew this was a make-or-break moment. She opened the door and forced herself to step outside. She might be crazy, but she was going to the fair.

It was only an hour drive to Warren. Marilyn parked the car in a diagonal space along the square that surrounded the courthouse in downtown. The building, nested in a grove of trees, was a massive three-story stone structure with a copper-topped dome that must have been built over a hundred years before.

"I guess this is it," she said.

"According to the flier, the Comfort Inn is somewhere around here," Karen said.

"Are you sure you're ready to do this?"

Karen opened the car door. "As ready as I'm going to be."

It was a comfortable, sunny day with white clouds dotting the sky. They walked the length of the square before Karen spotted the hotel, another three-story brick building from a previous century. If it hadn't been for the cars and modern signage, she might have thought they'd been transported back to the early 1900s.

By the time they reached the front doors, Karen's heart was racing. Maybe this was a bad idea. What was a social worker doing at a psychic fair? She dealt with people with psychoses and mental problems. Their issues were clear-cut in most instances. She knew Joe wasn't talking to Jesus, and Mike wasn't a secret agent. But what about her? Was she suffering from some sort of mental illness herself?

"You going in?" Marilyn stood holding the door.

Karen saw her reflection in the glass door. She reminded herself of Dr. Moody's book. She wasn't the only one who'd experienced a connection with a world beyond our own. If she backed out now, she'd never know.

"Yes," she said, stepping over the threshold. "Let's go."

The hotel lobby was packed with people of all ages. Most of them looked normal, but there were a few hippy types with long skirts, scarves, and colored hair. Karen joined a line leading to the registration table. Mom was probably scowling at her from the other side. *Did I teach you nothing, Karen? What are you doing here? You are going straight to hell.* Obie, on the other hand, would be happy she was taking this road.

"Hi," a brunette with wire-rimmed glasses greeted her at the registration table. She handed Karen a flier that listed events and vendor locations. "Welcome to the Psychic Fair. Would you like to sign up for a reading?"

"A reading?"

The woman pointed to a row of clipboards with sign-up sheets. "Readings are ten dollars for a twenty-minute session. You can pick anyone you'd like and sign up for a time."

Karen turned back to Marilyn. "What do you think?"

"I think that's what you came for," Marilyn said. "Pick a time."

Karen glanced over the sheets. Psychometry. Angel Psychic. Medium. Tarot Readings. She had no idea who to select. *Sharon. Psychic Medium.* Karen signed on the line for 11:00 am and retrieved her wallet from her backpack.

"Do you want to sign up?" she asked Marilyn.

"No," Marilyn said. "I'll just check out the vendors."

Karen handed the woman a ten-dollar bill and she received a card with the time and the woman's name on it.

"You could sell your art here," she said to Marilyn.

Marilyn shrugged. It had been years since she'd done any airbrush art. Their days of traveling to car shows were far behind them. Karen still missed it sometimes. Marilyn had moved on with her life.

"I've got about half an hour," Karen said. "Let's check out the place."

The vendors' room was almost as crowded as the lobby. Karen followed the crowd past tables covered with therapy candles, crystals, pagan supplies, and magical jewelry. Her mind whirled. She'd seen plenty of strange people at the county fairs: tarot readers, men on stilts, high-wire acrobats. This was an entire world she never knew existed.

"Hi," a petite woman with long hair said. "How are you today?"

"Fine," Karen said. She wasn't fine. She felt a bit sick.

"Is this your first time at the psychic fair?"

Karen nodded.

"I'm Jackie," she said. "I practice Rachi healing. My husband discovers past lives."

"Oh." Karen glanced at the woman's bracelet display. The pieces were made from a variety of crystals.

As they talked, the woman explained how she had been a chemist working for a large chemical company until she was in an accident. Now she made bracelets. Karen found a moonstone and amethyst piece that she liked and bought it.

"It's almost time for your reading," Marilyn said.

Karen checked her watch. "You're right."

Readings were held in an adjacent room. At 11:00, the doors

opened. People with earlier appointments exited. Karen followed others into the room. She checked her card and glanced at the various tables decorated with tablecloths, candles, crystal balls, and other trappings. *Sharon.* Karen found the woman sitting at a round table near the back of the room. She looked unusually normal, salt-and-pepper hair, dressed in a blouse and pants, no flowered hippy dress, crystal pendants, or black candles.

Karen sat.

"Welcome," Sharon said. She placed her hands face up on the table. "This your first time to receive a reading?"

"Yes," Karen said. "I've never been here before."

Sharon smiled and her warmth radiated outward. Karen relaxed a bit.

"That's okay," Sharon said. "It's nothing to be nervous about."

"Yeah," Karen said. But she was nervous. What was she getting herself into?

"What's your name?"

"Karen."

Sharon nodded and took a deep breath.

"Well, Karen, I see that you have a psychic gift," Sharon said. "You've had that gift from very early on in your life. It's been dormant for many years."

Karen nodded. The woman couldn't possibly know that. Maybe it was a good guess. Or maybe she was a real psychic.

"You are very intuitive," Sharon said. "I see you beginning this work in six months."

Six months! That was crazy. She was just here to check things out. There was no way she would become a psychic. She had a job and a husband and a reputation to maintain. New Castle was the last place a person would want to become a psychic. She would be a laughingstock in the community.

"I see you retiring and doing this type of work full-time," Sharon said.

Karen had wanted to find a way to help people. She wasn't sure what she expected to hear from this woman, but she certainly didn't want to find out she should become a psychic reader.

"You have a strong connection," Sharon said.

"Thanks," Karen mumbled. This was crazy.

"Look," Sharon said. "Let me get you connected with Charlotte Moore. She can get you information on the SCOPE meetings."

SCOPE. What kind of organization was that? What had she gotten herself into? Where was Marilyn? They should get out of there.

Sharon waved at Charlotte to come to the table. Karen soon found that SCOPE was a senior center on the opposite side of the square. A psychic group held meetings there on Wednesday evenings. Charlotte wrote the information down on a piece of paper and handed it to Karen. "Stop by on Wednesday," she said. "I'll introduce you to everyone."

"Thanks," Karen said.

"Our time is up," Sharon said. Two men opened the doors to the room. "It was good to meet you."

"Yeah," Karen said. She'd never been so anxious to leave a place.

Karen found Marilyn listening to a talk on angels in one of the meeting rooms and sat in a chair next to hers.

"How did it go?" Marilyn asked.

"You won't believe it," Karen whispered. She told her about the reading and the suggestion to go to the SCOPE meeting.

"Do you want to go?" Marilyn asked.

"I don't know."

"This is what you wanted, wasn't it?"

"Yes," Karen said. "But …"

"No buts," Marilyn said. "We might as well go."

* * *

Karen followed Marilyn up the sidewalk to the SCOPE center. The modern one-story brick building was nestled in the trees near the river. Karen felt more relaxed than she had at the psychic fair. They found the meeting of the Trumbull County Society of Psychic Research was held in the main meeting hall of the senior center.

About thirty people sat around tables in the room. Karen and Marilyn sat together. Karen wasn't ready to socialize but watched as others did so. After a few moments, a speaker was introduced. That evening talk was about medical intuitive mediumship. Karen wondered about being a medium. That seemed more substantial than doing psychic readings. She preferred the idea of being a bridge between this world and the spirit world beyond.

After the meeting, she browsed through fliers on a table at the side of the room. One caught her eye: *Demonstration of Mediumship with Reverend Leonard Young.* It was being held at a Days Inn in New York State somewhere.

"This looks interesting," she said to Marilyn.

"Mediumship," Marilyn said. "Isn't that talking to spirits?"

"Yeah," Karen said. "I think so."

Marilyn shrugged. "It won't hurt to see what it's all about."

CHAPTER 25

NOVEMBER 1917: A WORLD AT WAR

Annie laid the corned beef brisket in a large kettle atop the stove, fat side up, dusted it with pepper and added bay and thyme. Agnes worked at the counter, chopping celery, carrots, and onions. This kitchen was roomier than the one in the house with the two old widows. Daniel had been right to move here. Raymond and Violet were older, and having three bedrooms gave them all more space.

Agnes carried the cutting board to the stove and slid the vegetables into the pot.

"All we need is potatoes." She ran a hand along her side and arched her back. Now that she was six months along, her pregnancy was starting to show.

Annie rinsed her hands in the sink and wiped them on her apron. "I'll get them," she said.

The stone cellar gave them lots of room for food storage. She had more than one hundred jars of canned fruits and vegetables neatly lined on the shelves. But every time it rained, she still worried about flooding.

Agnes was sitting at the table when Annie returned to the kitchen. Annie lifted her apron and let the potatoes roll into the sink. "Are you feeling ill?"

"It's just my back," Agnes said.

Annie washed the potatoes and began to cut them into chunks. "I think it's time you tell everyone about the marriage before that babe is born." Ross Guthrie was a tall, good-looking man, with a square jaw and wavy hair. Annie was proud to call him son, even if his parents wouldn't be happy to find out about the marriage.

"I know," Agnes said. She and Ross had eloped to Brooks County, West Virginia, in January. Here it was, halfway into November, and they still hadn't made an official announcement. "But I don't want to spoil Dad's anniversary party tonight."

"I understood when you didn't want to spoil Mabel's wedding in April, but you've had plenty of time since then. Your dad won't mind you announcing the news." Annie scooped the potatoes into the pot and slid the heavy lid into place. "Mrs. Guthrie may not want her precious son married to a Spiritualist, but she's just going to have to accept it. I'm sure she suspects something by now anyway."

"I suppose you're right."

"We had our largest rally and revival ever this year," Annie said. "Your dad even convinced the Maccabees Lodge to attend on a Sunday. We are starting to be respected in town. Ross can't worry about his mother's opinion. He's a grown man."

Annie opened the oven door and slid the pot inside. "Believe me. Once Mrs. Guthrie knows there's a little one on the way, it won't matter if you're a Hindu Yogi Fire Dancer from India, you'll be part of the Guthrie family."

Agnes laughed. "You're right. We'll make the announcement tonight."

* * *

Annie tried not to pay too much attention to the war in Europe. That was Daniel's job. He'd kept track of every battle and troop movement since the conflict began in 1914 with the assignation of Archduke Ferdinand. When Germany invaded Luxembourg and Belgium, he paced the length of the house grumbling. After British forces moved into France, he complained it was just a matter of time before the United States joined the war. The sinking of the *Lusitania*, which killed over one hundred Americans, made everyone angry. But the United States didn't declare war on Germany until April of 1917, right before Mabel's wedding.

Despite the call to war and enlisted men parading down

Washington Street, Annie was still able to keep the conflict out of her mind for a while. When thousands of boys began dying, she couldn't ignore it any longer. Every week they had newcomers at the church looking for a way to contact their lost boys, looking for peace of mind.

Still, her own family remained unscathed. At least until Ross Guthrie brought the fighting right to her doorstep. It hadn't even been a month since they announced their marriage and the upcoming birth of their child when he broke the news. "I've enlisted in the army."

"The army?" Daniel puffed on his pipe and glared at Agnes. Annie held her tongue. Ross hadn't been drafted. She was livid.

"It's my patriotic duty," Ross said.

"But what about the baby?" Annie said.

"We've talked it over," Agnes said.

"I've joined the aviation group," Ross said. "I won't be on the front lines. Besides, I want our child to live in a world without war."

"So, you'll be doing what? Flying a plane?"

"No," Ross said. "I'll be sending up observation balloons."

"Hmm," Daniel said. "I suppose it's too late to stop you."

"It'll be fine, Dad," Agnes said. "I know it."

Agnes had a deep connection with the spirit world. She insisted that the war would be over before Christmas of next year and that Ross would be safe. Annie wasn't so sure. It was one thing to speak with the spirits and another to predict the future. She hoped Agnes was right.

* * *

With Ross away, the January snow seemed deeper than usual. But that did not detract from church attendance. After Sunday evening services, Raymond helped Daniel and Edward clear the extra chairs from the back of the room. Annie gathered her sermon notes and Lydia counted money from the collection plates.

Agnes ambled across the room with Violet in tow. "Are we going to need those chairs for Mrs. Ashton's funeral?"

"I don't think so," Annie said. "That reminds me. Danny, did you ever hear back from Mr. Altar?"

"You don't see any new chairs, do you?"

Mr. Altar was one of the wealthiest men in the city. It had been almost a month ago when he'd come to Daniel for healing. He was so happy that his chest pain and swollen legs had subsided that he promised Daniel he'd donate whatever they needed. When Daniel suggested one hundred new folding chairs, he'd agreed.

"So much for being a man of his word," Daniel said. "I'll not be helping him again."

Lydia placed the money in her change bag. "This will give us enough to buy the Beckwith organ," she said. "Unless you would rather buy more chairs."

"No," Annie said. "We've been saving for the organ for a long time."

Lydia nodded. "We can put that on the next agenda. And I intend to nominate you as minister."

"You know how I feel about that," Annie said. The church was growing, and she felt they needed to become a member of an official organization if they were to be accepted in the city as a real church. She wanted to be ordained before calling herself a minister and had suggested they join the National Spiritualist Association of Churches. The organization formed in 1893 and was affiliated with the Morris Pratt Institute in Milwaukee and the Center for Spiritualist Studies in Lily Dale. Lydia, on the other hand, wanted to remain independent. The board was evenly split over the idea.

Even with their differences, Annie was elected as minister at their mid-January meeting. By then, Ross was a private stationed at Camp Lee Hall, Newport News, Virginia. Agnes decided to visit her sister Mabel in Salem, Ohio, before it was time for the baby to arrive. By February, Ross had moved to Waco, Texas. Agnes gave birth at Mabel's home and had a healthy baby girl, Virginia.

The war consumed their every waking hour. Ross was assigned to the 23rd Balloon American Expeditionary Force (AEF) under the command of General Pershing. He came home in July on a five-day furlough from Camp Lee Hall, Newport News, and then was sent to France. The AEF fought alongside the French, British, Canadians, and Austrians, as well as the Italian army. They helped the French on the Western Front during the Aisne Offensive that summer.

Daniel read the papers aloud to Annie every day. On Sundays, she was overwhelmed by mothers and fathers trying to reach the spirits of the young men who'd died in the terrible war. David, Warren, Francisco, Mike. They were at peace in the spirit world, but their families still grieved. The boys had been too young to die. War was a terrible thing.

Agnes was busy on Wednesday nights with her trance messages. More and more people attended. Soon they were lifting tables during seances. Annie was glad that the church was able to help so many, but all the healing seemed to be taking a toll on Daniel. He never complained.

As summer turned to fall, the AEF fought in the battle of Saint-Mihiel and the Meuse-Argonne Offensive. Some of the balloon squadrons were at the front, but they didn't know which ones. Every time Annie saw Agnes holding little Virginia, she prayed that Ross would return home safe. The only news they'd heard was that it was the bloodiest campaign for the AEF.

When the war ended on November 11, 1918, everyone breathed a sigh of relief. Ross's parents received a letter from him in December and reported it to the paper. Agnes read the article to them:

"Time is hanging heavily on his hands since the armistice was signed and that he is spending as much time as possible in seeing the sights. Part of the country in which he is stationed is an almost Adam-less Eden, as all Frenchmen are at the front with the army except those who are dead or in hospitals. He is especially interested in certain ancient buildings concerning which he studied in his history lessons in school days. Nothing is known as to when he will be able to come home, but he longs for the day and expresses the hope that his homeward passage will be on a large vessel, thus reducing his chances of becoming seasick."

"See, Dad," Agnes said. "I told you Ross would be fine."

"Thank, God," Daniel said. "The spirits protected him."

CHAPTER 26

AUGUST 2004: THE ENGLISH MEDIUM

It was a two-hour drive from New Castle to the Days Inn in Fredonia, New York. Karen was glad to have Marilyn with her for moral support, because the closer they got to the town, the more nervous she became. It was one thing to visit a psychic at a fair, and quite another to attend a class to become a medium. She remembered Father Daugherty praying at Dad's funeral. What would he think if he saw her now? What kind of Catholic would forsake her faith to talk to spirits?

Karen exited Interstate 90 at the Fredonia/Dunkirk exit and followed the ramp to a light.

"Turn left here," Marilyn said. "It should be on the right-hand side."

They passed fast-food restaurants and turned onto a narrow road leading back to the hotel. The one-story building was white brick and looked more like a warehouse than a hotel.

"I guess this is it," Karen said. It seemed like a strange place to hold classes. Why would a trained medium pick a hotel off the highway in upstate New York? They were out in the middle of nowhere.

Karen turned off the engine and opened the car door. August heat flooded in. She fought the urge to start the car and return home.

The hotel's main lobby was plain, but clean. The woman at the counter had reservations waiting for them and told Karen where the classes would be held. Their room was just a few feet down the main hall, and they had a couple of hours to kill before the Friday evening class began.

"Do you want to get something to eat?" Marilyn asked.

"No," Karen said. "I'm not hungry. You can eat if you want."

"You sure?"

"I'm going to rest a bit."

Marilyn shrugged. "I'll be back before your class starts."

Karen lay on the bed near the window and closed her eyes, but she couldn't sleep. She turned on the TV and tried to listen to the news. They were still talking about Martha Stewart going to jail. The New Jersey governor had come out as a gay man, and a hurricane was bearing down on Florida. Wonderful. She turned the TV off and looked out the window. There was nothing to see but parking lots.

After pacing the length of the room a few times, she removed the flier from her backpack. Reverend Leonard Young. He had a normal-sounding name and he was a reverend, but what if he was one of those woo-woo people? There wasn't any mention of tarot cards, crystals, or magic potions on the flier, but if he advertised at the psychic fair, he might use all that stuff.

Marilyn returned with a bag from Kentucky Fried Chicken and a glass of Coke. "I thought you were going to rest," she said.

"I tried," Karen said. "I'm too nervous. What if this isn't the right thing to be doing?"

Marilyn sat on the bed and slid a box out of the bag. The chicken did smell good, but Karen's stomach twisted at the thought of eating.

"No one can force you to stay," Marilyn said. "If you don't like the class, we can leave."

"Yeah," Karen said. "I suppose you're right."

* * *

Karen entered the hotel meeting room. Twenty rows of chairs faced a podium at the far end, but there were only two women seated near the front. Behind the podium, an older man with receding gray hair and glasses adjusted his blue tie. Karen walked to the front feeling self-conscious, sat in the second row, and placed her backpack on the chair beside her. A man and three other women joined them a few minutes later and sat across the aisle.

"Well," the man at the podium said with an English accent. "I think everyone is here. To start, I'd like to introduce myself. I'm Reverend Leonard Young, a Spiritualist minister and a member of the Spiritualist National Union of Great Britain. I've taught mediumship at Arthur Findlay College and will cover many of the basics of mediumship with you this weekend."

There was an organization and a college? Maybe this wouldn't be too bad. Karen slid a notebook from her bag and searched for a pen.

"Mediumship requires development, direction, and most of all dedication," Reverend Young said. "In this class, you will learn the history of Spiritualism, the fundamentals of mediumship, and we will discuss issues such as psychic science, poltergeists and hauntings, and prophesy."

Karen scribbled notes as fast as she could.

Reverend Young began with the history of Spiritualism. He told them it began with a small cabin in a rural town in western New York, not far from where they were holding the class. In December of 1847, the Fox family rented the house. They were frequently disturbed at night with the sounds as of furniture being moved or knocking on the doors and walls. After the initial events in Hydesville, Margaret and Catherine were sent to Rochester to live with their sister, Leah Fish. Their ability to communicate with spirits through rapping sounds continued and they became well-known mediums in the area.

Spiritualism bloomed in the late 1800s. Karen took notes as fast as she could. Reverend Young mentioned Emma Hardinge Britten, William Stanton Moses, William Eglinton, and more. He also mentioned spirit artists like the Bangs Sisters. There were physical mediums who produced ectoplasm and objects, trance mediums with spirit guides, healing mediums, spirit art and photography. Karen could barely keep up. She felt like she was back in college. There was much more to Spiritualism than she imagined. She was surprised to find that it was a religion with organizations in both the United States and Great Britain. This definitely wasn't a *woo-woo* class.

After a short break, Reverend Young informed them they were going to try their first exercise.

"We are going to start small," he said. He explained that the basic goal of the exercise was to open one's mind to others. He glanced at the students. Karen felt her heart pounding. Don't pick me, she thought. Don't pick me.

"You," he said, pointing to Karen. "Get up here."

Karen laid her notebook on the chair. Oh, no, she thought. She had no idea how to "open her mind."

"Come on," Reverend Young said.

Karen joined him at the podium. "I don't know how to do this," she said.

"Good," he said. "I like them raw."

Karen breathed deeply. This wasn't going to go well.

Reverend Young pointed to a woman in the group. "I want you to tell me something about her."

Karen felt her face flush.

"Whatever comes to your mind," Reverend Young said. "Just go with it."

"Um." Nursing, Karen thought. Could that be right? "Healthcare," she said. "She works in healthcare, is married, and has kids."

The reverend pointed to the woman. "How did she do?"

"She's right," the woman said. "I'm a nurse and married with kids."

The reverend nodded. "Good job," he said. "You can take your seat."

Karen breathed a sigh of relief. But she didn't like being put on the spot. She hoped this wasn't going to be a regular occurrence in the class.

* * *

Saturday morning began with lectures. Karen was happy to

be taking notes and listening. Just as she thought the day would be only lectures, Reverend Young insisted they try another technique to contact spirits this time.

"I expect you to find out if the spirit was a man or woman first," he said. "Then I want you to find out the person's name and how they died."

He called on a woman named Trudy first. She'd said she was a pet psychic earlier that day. Karen wondered if the ability was general enough that she could talk to spirits too. Trudy was assigned another woman in the room. She didn't get a name for the spirit but identified it as the woman's mother.

Karen hoped Reverend Young wouldn't notice her, but how could he not? There were only eight people in the class. It didn't take long for the demonstration to come to her.

"Your turn," Reverend Young said. "Karen, isn't it?"

"Yes," she said. Her stomach fluttered.

"Join me." He took her by the hand and pointed to a woman in the front row. "Man or woman?"

Karen breathed deeply. She saw an old man in her mind. "Man," she said. "Grandfather."

"Okay," he said. "How did he die?"

She felt a pain in her chest but didn't know if that was the spirit talking or her nerves. "Heart problems."

The woman nodded.

"Is that correct?" the reverend asked.

"Yes," she said.

"Name?" he asked Karen.

Name. Name. How was she supposed to know his name?

"Name?" he repeated.

"Arthur," she said.

"That's right!"

How did she know that? Was it really that simple to connect with the spirits? She'd known the spirits were out there for years but didn't expect contacting them would be anything like this.

Reverend Young squeezed her hand. "Good, Karen. That's enough for now."

When they finally broke for lunch, Karen's back was a knot

of pain. She strode stiffly to her hotel room and dropped her backpack beside the bed.

"How was it?" Marilyn asked. "Are you ready for lunch?"

"My back is killing me," Karen said.

"Your back? You'd better lie down." Marilyn helped her onto the bed. "When did this start?"

"Just a little while ago." Karen lay back. "Oh man," she said. "Nothing like this has ever happened to me before."

"Just relax," Marilyn said.

"I'm trying." Karen closed her eyes. "I think it's the stress."

"Maybe you shouldn't go back."

"No," Karen said. "I'm learning a lot. I can't quit now."

* * *

The pain in her back eased enough that she could attend the afternoon session. When she returned to the room, she found Marilyn on the bed watching TV.

"How's your back?" Marilyn asked.

"Better," Karen said. "Get ready. We're going out for dinner."

"Oh," Marilyn said. "I hope it's not someplace fancy."

"It's at a medium's house at a place called Lily Dale."

"Lily Dale? What's that?"

"I have no idea. Reverend Young invited the whole class. I think we should go."

"It's okay with me, but I thought you didn't like driving after dark."

"Reverend Young said it's not far, just up the road."

They followed Reverend Young's directions and took a road from town that followed the edge of a lake. Karen turned left and drove over a bridge that led to a white guard booth with brick posts on either side. A blue sign hung over a gate beyond the booth.

"Lily Dale Assembly," Marilyn read. "World's largest center for the Religion of Spiritualism."

They stopped at the gate and Karen rolled down the window. The woman inside asked if they had a pass.

"No," Karen said. She paid the fee. "We are looking for the house of Janet Nohavic on Cleveland Avenue," Karen said.

"Turn right," the woman said. "Then it's the second road to your left."

"Thanks."

Karen drove by a grassy park and found herself in a little village of small homes. The medium's house was on the right side of the road, just as Reverend Young had indicated.

"This is it," she said. The house had a screened-in front porch that overlooked the lake.

"Nice place," Marilyn said.

"Yeah." Karen opened the car door and hesitated. Reverend Young was a nice man, but she wasn't sure she was ready to meet another medium. Her stomach turned as they walked up the steps and went through the screen door onto the porch. They were greeted by a heavy-set woman. Her hair was short and fine bangs covered her forehead.

"Welcome," she said. "I'm Janet."

"I'm Karen, and this is my friend Marilyn. We're from Reverend Young's class."

"Come in," Janet said. The entrance led to the dining room. A large table was set to accommodate at least a dozen people. Janet introduced them to two other women, Carol and Sharon. Reverend Young hadn't told the class there was going to be a houseful of mediums. Karen spotted the reverend in the living room with another man, another medium she assumed. What were they doing here?

It wasn't long before the food was ready. Karen sat across from Reverend Young and his colleague, Alex. Janet had cooked brisket on the grill with potatoes and vegetables. She followed the delicious meal with pies for dessert. Karen almost forgot her nervousness.

After the meal, cool air blew in off the lake and people stayed to talk. Karen found herself next to Janet.

"Have you been a medium for a long time?" Karen asked.

"No," Janet said. "You could say it's my second calling."

"Oh," Karen said. "What were you before."

"I was a nun."

Karen glanced at Marilyn. She'd heard it too. A nun? Karen couldn't believe it. She had spent her whole life trying to be a good Catholic. She'd worried about giving up her faith to become a medium, and she was just a church member, not an ordained nun. If Janet could make a leap like that, why not her? She was in. Whatever it took, she would be a good medium. This would be her new life.

CHAPTER 27

APRIL 1920: UNIONS BROKEN

Annie and Lydia walked along East Washington Street, skirting a crowd that had gathered outside Clutton Drug. It was mid-April, but the morning air was still cool. There were no black clouds belching into the sky and, except for a passing trolley or car horn, the city was unusually quiet.

"Is Edward at work today?" Annie asked.

"Yes," Lydia said. "The local leaders said there wouldn't be a strike here."

The railroad strike had been spreading across the country. Yardmen from different railroads were refusing to work in New Castle. Transportation was in chaos. The Loyal Order of the Moose had opened their hall for meetings and Mayor Newell assured everyone that coal delivery to the water company and hospitals would not be interrupted. Carnegie Steel New Castle Works and Shenango Tin Mill were both closed. Workers hung out at the Greek coffee houses and congregated at the taverns playing cards. The hardware stores had a run on shovels, hoes, and wallpaper. Wives appeared to be putting their husbands to work at home on their days off.

"Danny hasn't worked in days," Annie said. "We won't have money to pay the bills if this keeps up."

"Edward heard the strike will break in Chicago soon."

Annie entered the door beside the drugstore and walked to the stairs. "It seems there's a strike somewhere every week. Can't the mill owners see we're struggling to feed our families?"

"It's a travesty," Lydia said. "It's the mill owners who control the city, paying off the politicians, the police, and the press. You can't trust any of them."

The Amalgamated Association of Iron, Steel and Tin Workers strike the previous year had lasted from September of 1919 until January of 1920. In New Castle, nearly five hundred workers met at Hobart Street to shut down the hot mill on September 21st. On the twenty-fourth, one hundred picketers started a riot. Stones were thrown, and Patrolman Fred Shuller was injured. Officer John Edwards was beaten so badly, he died. Sophie Johnson was shot. The newspaper had blamed "foreigners" from Youngstown, but Daniel had been part of the crowd and said they were all local boys.

"I told Edward the rail workers should join the strike, but he doesn't like to rock the boat."

"We're at their mercy," Annie said. "Strike and don't get paid. Maybe get put in jail."

State police were called in after the September riot. They swore in one hundred deputies to control the workers. Mayor Newell came out against the strike saying he didn't want any more nonsense in the city. The chief of police arrested over one hundred people the first week and held at least forty of them as "suspicious persons" until the strike was over. The state police brutalized the strikers. Thank goodness, Daniel hadn't been involved in any of that.

Just as the steel strike was cooling down, some 400,000 members of the United Mine Workers went on strike in November. The attorney general of the United States invoked the Lever Act, criminalizing the workers' interference with the production and transportation of necessities. Coal operators spread rumors that the strikers were working for Russian communist leaders Lenin and Trotsky.

It's not that Annie didn't want Daniel to earn more money or have an eight-hour workday instead of twelve. She's sure his health would be better if he wasn't working himself into an early grave. She wished the unions would succeed, but it seemed there was a terrible price to pay. She didn't want to be a widow with two children still at home.

Annie followed Lydia up the stairs. Rent for the church was cheaper in this building than in the old place, but Annie didn't like it as well. The room wasn't as large. She expected that their event scheduled for Thursday evening would be overcrowded. Dr. Lee of Homestead was a well-known healer, and Professor and Mrs. Rogan were gifted musicians. They had set a time for healings earlier in the afternoon but were still expecting lots of people at the main event.

Lydia opened the door to the meeting room. A cool draft wound around them. Annie shivered.

"Charley says we should set up as many chairs as we can fit," Lydia said.

Annie didn't need Charley to tell her that, but she might need his help to convince Lydia about her other idea. She removed her coat and hat and hung it over the dais. Lydia joined her, placing her hat at the top of the stack.

Annie cleared her throat. "I know I've mentioned this before," she said, "but I think it's time we form an official church."

"This is an official church," Lydia said.

"I didn't mean it that way."

Lydia strolled to the side of the room, opened the closet, and removed two wooden folding chairs.

"I think it's time for a charter. We need to incorporate."

"Why?" Lydia opened each chair and set it before the dais. "We are Spiritualists, not Presbyterians or Catholics. And we certainly don't need the government telling us what to do."

"That's just my point," Annie said. "When you were arrested for fortune-telling, you testified that you were a Spiritualist, but how many had ever heard of such a thing? Your lawyer had to explain to them what a medium was. Mrs. Becker and Mrs. Peebles had to testify that your religion was real."

"That was over ten years ago. Things have changed." Lydia stomped to the closet, cheeks red. She returned with two more chairs.

"Things have not changed as much as you think," Annie said.

"I still oppose the idea," Lydia said. "I don't need someone's permission to seek the truth."

"That's not what I'm saying."

"If you are so determined," Lydia said, "bring it up at the board meeting."

"I think I'll do that." Annie couldn't understand why Lydia was so stubborn. Being a member of a larger organization wouldn't take away her freedom. If anything, it would give her more by giving them all more legitimacy.

Two weeks later, the board voted on the proposal. Annie, Daniel, Agnes, Elizabeth Thomas, and Thomas Grant applied for a charter for the Spiritual Church of Truth. Lydia accepted their decision but wasn't happy. A few weeks later, she decided to leave the church. She rented out a room in the city building and opened The Spiritual Church of the Soul.

Annie missed not having Lydia at their meetings, but Agnes assured her that it was for the best. Everyone needed to grow spiritually in their own way. "Now that the baby is older, I can help more," she said. "I have decided to stop worrying about what Ross's parents think. I want to begin doing readings."

CHAPTER 28

SUMMER 2005: THE ART OF MEDIUMSHIP

After Karen's first class with Leonard, she committed herself to becoming a medium. She planned to take more classes at the Days Inn but found that Leonard would be teaching his more advanced sessions at the Journey Within, a Spiritualist church in New Jersey founded by the medium she'd met at Lily Dale, Janet Nohavec. Janet had a real church.

On the long trip to New Jersey with Marilyn, Karen thought of all the classes she would need before becoming a full-fledged medium. As the PA Turnpike crested the Appalachian ridge, she imagined having a little office to work out of where she could see clients privately. She'd be like the mediums at Lily Dale.

"You're being awful quiet," Marilyn said.

"I'm thinking about opening a little office."

"An office? For what?"

"Mediumship," Karen said.

"You have a full-time job," Marilyn said. "Are you going to do readings in the evening? After work?"

"What's all the training for if I don't use it?" Leonard's advanced classes were grueling. He made sure his students were familiar with the philosophy and principles of Spiritualism. Between hands-on sessions, he would discuss noteworthy mediums, Emma Hardinge Britten, Harry Edwards, and Gordon Higginson, and seers of the past, Andrew Jackson Davis and

Arthur Findley. He taught his students how to prepare for private readings and public demonstrations.

"I didn't say you shouldn't use it," Marilyn said.

"Now that I know how to interpret symbols, I don't want to forget everything I've learned." Leonard stressed the importance of interpreting. A symbol could have multiple meanings, depending upon the spirit, the medium, and the situation. A bell, for example, could mean the name of a person or street, or represent an idea, or just be a bell that someone owns. "You know the old saying, use it or lose it."

"You're the one who is concerned about how the New Castle people are going to accept this," Marilyn said.

"I know." Karen was still torn about her decision. This might be the biggest mistake of her life.

After driving most of the day, the Pompton Lakes exit came into view. Marilyn followed the road past a lake and circled around to the Holiday Inn. It was a good place to stay. Fast-food places and stores were located near the exit. Janet's church was less than a mile down the road. They would have time to relax before her class began.

"Do you want to pick up something to drink?"

"Sure," Karen said. "But I don't want to waste too much time."

Leonard wouldn't take any excuses for tardiness. To be a good medium, one must follow protocol. Being timely and practicing were part of that regimen. You were working for the spirit world and not yourself. Leonard was clear. If you couldn't work for them, he didn't want you in his class.

As they waited in the drive thru, Karen reviewed the steps for readings in her head. When connecting with a spirit the medium must ask if it was a man or woman, its name, and how it died. Insisting on the same information created a strong bond with the spirit and allowed for a better reading. There was no room for ego. There were no short-cuts. You were a conduit to the spirits. It was your job to open yourself to their messages.

"Do you think taking these classes is a mistake?" Karen asked.

"I don't know," Marilyn said. "I guess you won't know if you don't try. You can't second-guess yourself, Karen.

Karen left Marilyn at the hotel and drove the short distance to the Journey Within church. The building reminded her of the Alamo, a Mexican mission-style structure with a stucco finish, flat roof, a peaked central roof embellishment, and double-door entrance flanked by two windows on each side. She parked the car in the side lot and joined the rest of the class in the main sanctuary. It was newly remodeled with an elevated platform behind the dais flanked by angels, both standing and kneeling. A frame hung on the center back wall, accentuating a stained-glass angel. The room was large enough to seat fifty comfortably and Karen heard they had been remarkably successful at attracting parishioners.

Karen sat in the front row, took out her notebook, and waited for Leonard to arrive. She recognized a few of the others from previous classes, including Janet Nohavec. It was never the same group present, but there were usually a dozen attending each class.

One woman she recognized from the traveling clairvoyance class. They learned that a trained medium can clearly see places and events at long distance, either in the physical dimension or in nonphysical dimensions. Leonard had years of experience as a trance medium, where the medium remains conscious while a spirit uses his mind to speak directly. Karen tried the technique but found it too difficult. Leonard assured the class that the development of a mediumship circle requires time, hard work, study, and, above all, patience. It would take months, maybe years, to develop the skills he taught them. Despite what many weekend courses promised, there was nothing "instant" about mediumship.

Another woman she knew from the aura class. Leonard taught that everything has an aura, which means it is surrounded by a field of its own energy. The ability to see auras is considered a psychic skill but it can be helpful when interpreting messages. Focusing on auras can also assist with spiritual healing and bringing harmony to a person's life. Karen wasn't really interested in auras, but it was good to know about them.

Leonard welcomed them to the class and informed them that this week they would be working on public demonstrations and trance mediumship. Karen was nervous about demonstrating in front of people, but if she was going to be a medium, maybe with her own church like this one, she would have to get used to it.

Leonard made going into trance look easy. He sat comfortably in a chair. Soon, his breathing slowed, and his face took on a peaceful demeanor. One of two spirit guides would speak. During this class, Leonard led the group by counting backward from one hundred. Karen struggled at first but found as she practiced it was easier to let go. She found herself walking along a cobblestone street in England. The sky was gray with smoke and the streets dirty and soot covered. The village was crowded with working-class folks, dressed in shabby garments. People talked with heavy accents.

When they came out of their trances, Leonard asked them what they had seen.

"I was in old England," Karen said. "In a village where people spoke with cockney accents."

"Cockney?" Leonard asked. Did he think she didn't know what a cockney accent was?

"Yes," she said. "I've heard people on TV speak with it." She wasn't dumb.

Leonard nodded and went on to the next student. Many had problems getting into trance. Again, Leonard urged them to practice. It was the only way they would become good mediums.

"Someday you'll be ready for physical mediumship," he said. Physical mediums could manifest loud raps and noises, voices, and materialize objects and spirit bodies, or body parts such as hands, legs, and feet. Karen didn't think she'd ever be ready for that.

* * *

At the end of the week, Leonard informed the class that there was going to be a public demonstration at the church. Karen returned to the hotel and told Marilyn about the event and the meal that was planned afterward.

"I don't think I want to go to the demonstration," she said.

"Why?"

"I'm tired."

Marilyn gave her that look out of the corner of her eye. They had been friends for too long. She knew Karen was lying. "That's not the reason."

Karen shrugged. She didn't want to tell Marilyn that she was terrified she might get called on.

"Leonard will be going into trance," Marilyn said. "I thought you said he was amazing."

"I did."

"I think you'd better go. You'll regret it if you don't."

Karen sighed.

"We'll sit in the back," Marilyn said. "You can leave anytime you want."

"Okay, okay," Karen said. "You've convinced me."

When they arrived at the church, the parking lot was almost full. Karen fought the urge to leave. She wanted to suggest they not go in, it was going to be too crowded, but Marilyn exited the car before she could get the words out. Karen felt more and more nervous as they neared the entrance. Marilyn held the door open for her and followed her inside. The sanctuary was over half full already.

"There are a couple of seats over there," Marilyn said, pointing to a group of empty chairs in the last row.

"Okay," Karen said. "We'll sit there." She waited for an older couple to move down the aisle.

"Karen," Reverend Sharon called from the front of the sanctuary. She motioned for Karen to come forward.

What does she want? Karen thought. Sharon was one of the ministers who helped Janet at the church. Karen had spoken to her several times. She was very friendly, and Karen liked her.

Karen inched her way through the crowd. Marilyn followed.

Sharon moved out of the circle of chairs that had been arranged at the front of the room. "Leonard wants you to be in the circle." She pointed to the chairs. "Have a seat."

"Me?" Karen said.

"Yes," Sharon said. "The both of you."

"Why do I have to go?" Marilyn whispered in Karen's ear.

Karen shrugged. "I'm sure they can tell you're gifted too."

"But I haven't taken any classes."

"That's what you get for convincing me to come to this," Karen said.

"Gee. Thanks."

Three women Karen had met from previous classes joined them in the circle, followed by Janet, Reverend Carol, and Reverend Sharon. Leonard sat across from Marilyn, and Janet sat across from Karen. Other members of Janet's church joined them. Karen felt her heart pounding in her ears. Sitting in front of a room of strangers was that last place she wanted to be. She prayed Leonard didn't call on her to do anything.

The room filled quickly. Janet stood, thanked everyone for coming, and introduced Leonard. She asked that they quiet down. Leonard would be going into trance and his spirit guide C.T. would be speaking to them through him. Karen had heard C.T. speak at one of her classes as well as Leonard's Irish spirit guide. She was relieved that the circle was focusing on Leonard. Maybe no one would notice she was there.

Leonard closed his eyes. Karen watched as his body relaxed. After a few minutes, the expression on his face changed. It was difficult to describe. He was still the round-faced, gentle-looking man she had grown to respect and appreciate, but his posture was straighter, his face more rigid, the aura about him stronger.

C.T. spoke to them now. His voice was like Leonard's but more forceful, deeper. He called Leonard his child, which had struck Karen as odd the first time she first heard it in Leonard's class. Now she realized C.T. saw them all as children, learning the lessons they would need before passing on to the spirit world.

C.T. addressed each person in the circle individually, giving them advice to help them walk their path in this life. Karen was overwhelmed with emotion. Her entire life she had felt out of place. It wasn't that she didn't love her family, they just didn't understand her need to connect with the spirit world. Sitting in the circle, she finally felt that she had found her place. Most of the people in the room were strangers, but she knew they understood her need.

"Karen," C.T. said through Leonard. "I want you to always follow your heart."

Tears came to her eyes. She nodded. "I will." She had spent her life helping others in the physical world. Now, she would give her life to the spirit world. Like Leonard, she would work for them.

Leonard turned to Janet. "And you will help her," C.T. said. "Of course," Janet said.

Karen was thankful that Janet would offer to help her, but she felt confident she could handle learning mediumship on her own. She would need more classes from Leonard to develop her techniques, but that wouldn't take long.

At the end of the demonstration, Leonard informed the audience that this would be his last demonstration before he retired. Karen was shocked. Despite his gruff exterior, she liked Leonard. He had an energy about him that put her at ease. His "just do it" attitude kept her going. She trusted him because he knew his stuff.

The circle group went out to eat at an Italian restaurant about fifteen minutes from the church. Everyone seemed to be enjoying themselves. When Leonard arrived, one of the women said, "Here comes the star."

"Don't say that," Karen whispered to herself. Hadn't he just spent the entire week telling them to keep their egos in check? Mediums were not stars. They worked for the spirit world.

Leonard sat across the table from Karen. Just her luck. She hoped he wouldn't accidently pick up on her thoughts. Karen didn't know if she was more sad or angry. How could Leonard just retire out of the blue like that? All the mediums she knew about had spent their entire lives working as mediums. She was sure Leonard was as good as they were. Why retire now? She was afraid to complain or ask. Instead, she fumed while the others chatted like nothing was happening.

After they ordered, Leonard leaned forward. "Heasley. Why

aren't you saying anything?"

"No reason," she said.

She ate only half of her spaghetti and thought about ordering some wine but decided against it. She held her tongue until the meal was over and she was seated beside Marilyn in the car.

"I don't know how I can finish my training without Leonard," she said. "Have I done all this for nothing?"

"There are other teachers," Marilyn said.

Karen shook her head. "But no one is like Leonard." Why would the spirits take her this far to abandon her?

"Give it some time," Marilyn said. "I think Leonard's retirement was a shock to everyone."

Karen didn't want to give it some time.

CHAPTER 29

MAY 1921: ORDINATION

Annie sat at the kitchen table and flipped through the newspaper. She wanted to buy a nice beef roast, but they were fifteen cents a pound. National Market had boiling beef for a third of that price. It would have to do. U.S. Steel was cutting wages across the country. In Youngstown, wages were down 5 percent at the tin mill. At some places, day laborers were taking home 20 percent less pay. Daniel had been waiting to hear news from the mill. A pay cut was better than no job, but he was angry that workers still had to struggle to live. Forming unions had worked to some degree, but companies fought back with police and Pinkertons. Workers had no choice but to knuckle under.

The front door creaked open.

"Hello," Agnes called out.

"In the kitchen," Annie said.

"Nanna." Virginia trundled down the hall in her pink coat and matching hat.

"Hi, precious," Annie said. It was difficult to believe that Raymond and Violet were in school and Virginia was walking. It seemed it was only yesterday when they were all babies. She lifted Virginia to her lap.

Agnes removed her hat and coat. "I wish this weather would warm up," she said. "It's awfully chilly for May. And it's not much warmer in this house."

"Saving on coal," Annie said.

"You don't want to catch your death," Agnes said.

"Nothing a sweater won't cure."

"I told you," Agnes said. "If you need some extra money, we will help you."

"You know how your father is."

"Ross is making good money."

"He's making money *now*," Annie said. Ross had been working for the Pennsylvania Company, handling freight at the West Washington Street depot for over a year. "You never know when there's going to be a strike." She knocked on the wooden table.

Virginia searched the pocket of Annie's apron for a cookie. It was empty. "How about some tea? The water on the stove should be hot enough."

"Did you know the boy who was hit by the motorcar?" Agnes emptied old tea from the pot, rinsed it, and added new leaves.

Annie shook her head. "He was only nine years old. Same age as Violet. I keep telling the kids to stay away from the street for just that reason." They had moved from Neshannock Avenue to Croton Street to get a better price on the rent. The new place sat beside the city tool house and Brown and Sons feed store. Motorcars came racing down the hill at all hours of the day and night. She was surprised there weren't more accidents.

"Did you read about the body of the young man they found in the Shenango River?" Agnes said.

"I don't think that was an accident. They said the body looked bruised, like he had been beaten."

"I think it was the same man whose spirit came to me at church two weeks ago. Sam. Do you remember? The one who drowned. No one at church recognized his name."

"The one tending pigs?"

"Yes," Agnes said. "He wanted me to tell his parents he was sorry. He was always a very good swimmer, but this time he drowned."

Agnes poured the tea and set a cup in front of Annie.

"I don't suppose you want to tell the police that information."

"No." Agnes chuckled. "I'm sure they'll discover the truth soon enough."

Victoria reached for Annie's cup. "Look in the pantry," Annie said to Agnes. "There might be a couple of cookies left in the tin." Agnes returned with a broken cookie. "Here, Ginny," she said. Virginia grabbed both pieces at once. "Have you heard back from Dr. Richardson?"

"Yes," Annie said. "He'll be taking the train from Lily Dale on the thirteenth. I have a room reserved at the Castleton Hotel for him."

"What about Lydia? Did you invite her to your ordination?"

"Yes," Annie said. "And I also invited Mrs. Comstock of the First Spiritualist Church and Mrs. Uber of the Progressive Truth Seekers."

"Pretty soon there will be a Spiritualist church on every corner," Agnes said.

"That's what I'm afraid of," Annie said. "Anyone can claim to be a Spiritualist."

"But we will lead the way with high standards and truth," Agnes said.

"Yes, we will."

* * *

Raymond and Ross moved tables to the edge of the meeting room. Daniel set up chairs. Annie covered the tables with white linens and arranged plates with cake and cookies that Lizzie Thomas and Nellie Ingram had made for the afternoon reception. Agnes had volunteered to bring the punch and punch bowl.

"How many chairs do we need?" Ross asked.

"Let's set them all up," Annie said. "I expect to fill the hall when Reverend Richardson speaks tonight."

Agnes entered the room carrying a large punch bowl and bag strung over her shoulder. Virginia toddled behind. "Oh, that's heavy," she said, letting the bag slide to the table.

"One of the men could have helped carry that," Annie said.

Agnes placed the bowl in the center of one table. "Did you see the paper?"

"No. Why?"

"I was right about the boy who drowned," Agnes said. "His name was Sam Paduanno. It was an accidental drowning, just like I said. And they had pigs."

Annie unpacked plates from home and stacked them next to the desserts. Agnes made the punch. The men arranged the last of the chairs.

"You should be getting ordained today too," Annie said to Agnes.

"I don't think I'm ready for that yet."

Ross slid a flask from the inner pocket of his jacket, took a sip, and offered it to Daniel.

"Don't mind if I do," Daniel said. He tossed his head back and took a swig. "Moving chairs is hard work." They both laughed.

"Don't let the cleaning lady see you with that," Agnes said. Detective Logan had been on a rampage since April. Three stills had been discovered, and their owners arrested. They even raided Mike Fazzone's house on Lutton Street and took his family's private wine.

"I guess you're against spiking the punch," Ross said.

"That's all we need is to have a raid printed on the front page of the newspaper," Annie said.

"I'm just joking."

"Leave your jokes for another time," Annie said. "And go fetch Dr. Richardson."

Ross returned with Dr. Richardson thirty minutes before the ceremony was supposed to begin. Richardson was a tall, well-spoken man with white hair and a calm aura about him. Annie had met him on one of her visits to Lily Dale where she discussed the problems of founding and maintaining a Spiritualist church in New Castle. As the president of the National Association of Psychics, he suggested the Spiritualist Church of the Truth join the organization. He'd also offered to ordain her.

"Good afternoon, Mrs. Johns," Richardson said. "This is a fine hall you have here."

The room was simple enough, with podium and wall hangings. "We meet every Sunday and Wednesday," Annie said. "The congregation is small but dedicated. But there are many with an interest in Spiritualism here in the city. Your lecture tonight will fill the room."

Dr. Richardson nodded. "This is a new beginning," he said. "Yes, it is."

CHAPTER 30

SUMMER 2007: FOLLOW YOUR HEART

After Leonard's retirement, Janet kept in touch. Karen took a few classes with her at Lily Dale. She kept remembering C.T.'s advice. *Follow your heart.* But she was torn about practicing mediumship. New Castle's first settlers were Presbyterians and Methodists. A beautiful gothic stone First Presbyterian Church stood as a monument to that history near the center of the downtown. In the early 1900s, Catholic immigrants arrived from Italy and eastern Europe to work in the mills. St. Mary's was the other large church in the city's center, looking like a miniature replica of Notre Dame. She couldn't compete with that.

What if she opened an office and no one came, or worse? Janet had had multiple problems buying and opening her church in New Jersey. She had tried to rent a building and the city council wouldn't let them open a church there. That led to a lawsuit, and they were forced to cancel the lease. She was left with thousands of dollars in legal costs. When she found a building to buy instead of rent, a parishioner promised $300,000 to purchase it. That led to another battle with the city, trying to convince them that she was opening a real church. New Castle and Pennsylvania were undoubtedly less progressive than New Jersey. Karen would have to be careful if she really wanted to follow her heart.

Karen had met a local psychic, Reverend Barbara, on one of her trips to the psychic fair in Ohio. Barbara was a teacher and counselor who promoted psychic fairs, workshops, and other metaphysical events and conducted private readings, weddings, and classes. She encouraged Karen to read at the fairs. Karen relented and read at a few benefits also, but it wasn't what she wanted to do.

Barbara suggested Karen be ordained. Barbara and a man named Cecil had established a small church near Akron. If she was ordained through their church, she could do readings at psychic fairs and be protected from lawsuits. Karen wasn't sure about their church, but she would at least be ordained and one step closer to being a real Spiritualist medium.

Karen and Marilyn drove out to Cecil's house. They discovered that their church only existed on paper. There wasn't a building. Cecil asked her a few questions, and just like that she was Reverend Karen Heasley. It was quite a contrast to Janet's organization. The Journey Within was a member of the British Spiritual National Union, was in a physical building, and from what Karen had seen, had more than fifty parishioners.

In the car on the way back home, Karen looked at the paper certificate.

"Are you happy now?" Marilyn asked. "You're official."

"I don't feel official. I could have just bought a certificate on-line."

"What do you want to do then?"

"I don't know." Karen sighed. "This isn't how I thought it would be."

"You've got another class with Janet next month. Why don't you ask her?"

"I will."

* * *

August in Lily Dale was hot. Karen was glad to be staying at Harmony House, which, unlike the main hotel, has window air conditioners. She'd stayed at the guest house a few times and was taken by the owners, Ellie and Tom Cratsely. Ellie was a wonderful stained-glass artist. Many of her pieces—angels, stars, wildlife—hung in their enclosed front porch. Tom had been teaching meditation and healing at Lily Dale for years. Karen was impressed by his knowledge. If she could obtain even a fraction of his expertise, she would be happy. Ellie and Tom walked the walk. She wanted to be like them and Janet.

On Saturday, Janet invited Karen and Marilyn to join her for dinner at the only restaurant in Stockton, a crossroads town with quant Victorian homes, a classic white church with a steeple, post office, fire department, and country store. The restaurant, which looked like an old two-story hotel with a full upstairs balcony and central turret, was the largest building in town.

After they ordered, Janet asked Karen how many private readings she had been doing.

Karen shrugged. She was embarrassed to admit that she had done only a few. "It's hard to do readings," she said. "I'm still working full-time." She was not going to mention that she was certified to be a minister from the church in Ohio. So much for following her heart.

"You need to decide if you are going to work for the spirit world or not," Janet said.

"I am," Karen said. "It's just …"

"Just what?" Janet said.

"I won't retire for four years."

"That's just an excuse."

Janet was right. If she was going to do this, she would have to commit herself to being a Spiritualist. The old Spiritualists didn't let things keep them from practicing, and in those days, they could be arrested and jailed in many places.

"Have you thought any more about opening a church?"

"No," Karen said. Even Janet hadn't opened a church right away. She started with a little shop and did readings there. Karen didn't know the first thing about churches. Just the thought of it made her stomach churn. "I don't think I'm ready for that."

"The spirits don't care if we are ready," Janet said. "They work in their own time."

Working for the spirits was one thing, but opening a church was a big endeavor. Janet didn't know New Castle and the people who lived there. A Spiritualist church could easily be labeled as a *woo-woo* place. People would spread all kinds of rumors and

Karen could be ostracized.

By the end of the meal, Karen wasn't convinced about opening a church. She certainly wouldn't be able to find a parishioner with thousands of dollars to help her out like Janet had. It would be better to wait a few years until after she retired. She wouldn't be under all the stress of working for social services and would then be able to dedicate her life to the spirit world full-time.

The following evening, Janet broached the subject again. She suggested that The Journey Within could sponsor the church and Janet could train Karen to be a minister under the SNU guidelines. Karen relented, agreeing to check out buildings in the New Castle area. If she found a place, she would take it as a sign that the spirits were behind her. If not, she'd go back to her small shop idea.

A week after they returned from Lily Dale, Karen noticed that there was a church for sale on Jackson Avenue. She called Marilyn.

"I think I found a church," Karen said.

"I thought you didn't want a church."

"It's not what I want. It's what the spirit world wants."

"Are you sure about this?"

"It won't hurt to look," Karen said. "Let's call the realtor and take a look at it."

"Sure."

They met the realtor in a residential section on the city's south side. The neighborhood seemed nice enough. The houses were small, and the yards well kept. The one-story church sat on a corner lot. It was neat and clean and looked like it might hold fifty people. The outside was covered with stucco, a red front door flanked by stained-glass windows made it look a bit like a church, but it was a gray, square box. The basement had rooms for Sunday school, but there weren't any pews in the sanctuary.

"There's not much parking," Marilyn said. There was probably enough space to park six or eight cars in the gravel that surrounded the building.

"And there isn't any property," Karen said. "The neighbor's driveway is right next to the building on the back side. And it's only six feet from the other neighbor's house."

"I don't like it," Marilyn said.

"Me either." New Castle had plenty of property for sale. "There has to be something better than this."

"You can always start the church in a house."

"No," Karen said. "If I start a church, I want a real church, not a religious center." She didn't want to be like the group in Ohio, holding meetings in someone's house.

Marilyn shrugged. "It's just a suggestion."

They drove by an old Christian church that was for sale on the corner of South Jefferson Street and Lutton Avenue. It was a more traditional church with a thirty-foot-high sanctuary, stained-glass windows, and meeting rooms. It was a beautiful building, but the only property was a strip of green between the building and the sidewalk. Everyone would have to find parking in the neighborhoods.

"It's not even worth looking at," Karen said. "I couldn't afford to heat it."

"I'm sure there are other churches around," Marilyn said.

"If the spirits want me to find a church," Karen said, "we will find something. If not, I can set up a little shop to sell spiritual things."

It wasn't two weeks later that Rod came home with some news for her. "Ron called me today," he said. "He was driving up Sheep Hill. There's a church up there that is going to be auctioned off."

"Sheep Hill?" That area was the old Polish section of the city when immigrants were arriving in the early 1900s to work in the mills. It was also home to Wasilewski's Market, which had just closed after being open for ninety-four years. They were famous for their kielbasas, sausages, hams, and other meats and had their own brand name, Wasilewski Sausage Makers.

"Do you want to see it?" Rod hadn't been thrilled about her idea to buy a church, but he was taking the idea in stride, just like he did her mediumship classes. If he'd been any other man, he might have thought his wife was going crazy and divorce her.

"Sure."

They followed the narrow road up the steep hill. A few houses stood beyond the crest. On the left, they found a small, one-story church and pulled into the gravel parking lot. The Pentecostal Church sign was still out front, but the church looked like it hadn't been used in years. The siding was in poor condition and there was only a single stained-glass window in the front.

"Well," Rod said, "what do you think?"

The church was in a residential neighborhood, but there were trees on one side, isolating it from the closest neighbors. The house on the other side of the parking lot was far from the building, and behind it was a wooded lot.

"Let's call the guy and see if we can look inside," she said.

The minister was a young man, in his thirties or forties. He met them at the church the next day and let them inside. The building was in worse shape than Karen expected. The sanctuary was covered in dark paneling. The carpeting was worn and dirty. Rod pointed out a section of the ceiling that was sagging.

"Needs some work," he said. All the utilities had been turned off, so they couldn't tell if the place needed any electrical or plumbing maintenance.

"It has pews," Karen said. If no one came to the auction, they could get a good price on it and be able to afford to renovate it.

The minister showed them the other rooms upstairs and guided them down the narrow stairway to the basement. The place looked like a cave, with dingy walls, two bathrooms that needed to be gutted, and a musty smell that enveloped everything.

"The auction is next week," the minister said.

Next week? That didn't give them much time to think about it. Only two months ago, Karen was worried about being ordained. Now she was buying a church. What was happening? She wanted the spirits to show her the way, but this was much too fast.

CHAPTER 31

OCTOBER 1927: THE TORCH IS PASSED

It was a cold afternoon, but even the smoke from the mills couldn't keep the October sun from glinting off the windows of passing motorcars. Agnes walked from the trolley stop up Croton Avenue to her parents' home. She had just enough time to remind Dad and Ray that they needed to help her set up the meeting hall for Saturday services and get back home to get the roast out of the oven. Ross's parents were coming for supper, and even though Ginny liked to help set the table, Agnes wanted everything to be perfect when they visited.

Agnes entered the house through the side door. The kitchen was overly warm with the oven on. Violet wore her long hair pulled back into a ponytail and was busy peeling potatoes at the sink.

"Where's Dad?" Agnes asked.

"Upstairs with Mom," Violet said. "She's sick."

"Sick?"

Agnes's first thought was of Mom's thyroid problem. The doctor had found a growth in her neck. There was talk of surgery at one point, but Mom didn't want to deal with that. Agnes hoped it wasn't an infectious disease. She was concerned about Ginny catching something, especially lately, with all the meetings going on in the city. Last week the Castleton Hotel opened and hosted a Red Cross conference with over one hundred people arriving from out of town. According to the newspaper, five hundred Boy Scouts and fathers were attending a banquet at the First Methodist

Episcopal Church that evening.

Agnes tossed her coat over a kitchen chair and rushed through the parlor to the stairs. Her boot heels clomped on the floor as she made her way up. Mom's cough echoed down the hall, a loud rasping sound. She found Dad sitting on the edge of the bed, squinting to read the label on a bottle of cough syrup.

Mom tried to speak but broke into a coughing fit instead. Probably not her thyroid, Agnes thought.

"Let me see that, Dad," Agnes said. "Aspironal. This is ten percent alcohol. You might as well use whiskey and honey."

"It's supposed to work," Dad said.

"It says to give one teaspoon. I suppose it isn't going to hurt." Agnes rounded the bed and put her lips to her mom's forehead. "A little fever. You'll not be reading tonight."

"You need to …" Cough. Cough.

"I'll take care of everything," Agnes said. "You get your rest."

Agnes found Ray laying on his bed reading. "Get your coat on," she said. "I need your help."

Ray was taller than Dad now and stretched the entire length of the bed. "What's going on?"

"Mom's ill," Agnes said. "You are going to have to run the service with me tomorrow."

"Sure, but …"

"Let's go," she said. "Now."

A few chairs were lined in neat rows from Wednesday's Truth Seekers meeting, so it didn't take them much time to set up everything. Agnes scanned the room. "Okay," she said. "That looks good. Plan on doing a majority of the readings."

On her way home, Agnes recalled dreams she'd been having since an Italian ocean liner sank off the coast of Brazil. Unlike the *Titanic*, the ship sank slowly and there was time to get rescue boats to the ship. Still, over three hundred people died in the incident. The night after the sinking, before she'd read news about it, she dreamed that spirits were hovering over a sinking ship, not knowing they had died. She hoped she wouldn't see ship's passengers at church later.

Supper with the Guthries was pleasant enough. Agnes was

careful not to mention she was doing readings that night. Ross's father had become less critical of their beliefs, mainly because of the news articles in the paper. The Spiritualists of Western Pennsylvania held their meeting at Cascade Park two years before. Reverend Morrow came up from Pittsburgh and was the principal speaker. Mrs. Massie and Mrs. Harley came up from Beaver Falls and Lydia Marquette assisted at the service. Over six hundred attended the event and Mr. Guthrie had been impressed by the numbers.

Last year, Dad stopped at the church on Sunday, not a usual habit with him since services were on Saturday evening. While there, he smelled something burning and called the fire department. The firemen discovered some old rags and brushes smoldering in the locked cupboard. Spontaneous combustion had burned a hole in the shelf. If he had not stopped by, the entire building would have burned. When Mr. Guthrie heard the story, he believed it was more than mere coincidence. But he wasn't ready to admit that Daniel had been led to the church by spirits.

Ross's mother held her ground. More than once, she mentioned the defamation lawsuit filed against Houdini by Mrs. Rose Sutcliffe, a Youngstown medium. Houdini claimed that all mediums were fakes and offered $10,000 to a charity if someone would show him a spirit manifestation that he couldn't reproduce by normal means. If Houdini called all mediums frauds, then it must be true. Sutcliffe was one of the fakes as far as Mrs. Guthrie was concerned. No doubt, she thought they were all going to hell, including her granddaughter, Ginny.

After supper, Agnes worked to rid herself of Mrs. Guthrie's negative vibrations. She meditated as she rode with Ross and Ginny on the trolley into town. When they exited onto East Washington Street, the sidewalks were overrun with Boy Scouts and their fathers, strolling the streets before making their way to the banquet on Mill Street. The Chocolate Shop attracted the largest crowd of window shoppers. Offutt's and Boston department stores were so crowded they looked like they were having sales. Men donned their hats as they exited United Cigar with boxes tucked under their arms. Even Clutton Drug was teeming with customers. Ross led the way through a group of uniformed boys to get to the side entrance.

Dad stayed home to tend Mom, while Ray took over the service. Nellie Ingram arrived early to get her music in place. Margaret Davis helped Ray with the readings. Agnes wasn't contacted by anyone from the sunken ship, much to her relief.

Ross, Violet, and Ray cleaned up after the service. Ginny gathered coins from the collection plate into a bag.

"Let's get home," Ross said. "We've all had a long day."

After they exited the room, Ross locked the door and followed them down the stairs. Agnes looked forward to fixing a nice hot cup of tea and resting, but the moment she exited the building onto the darkened street, she felt the urge to visit her mother.

"I need to check on Mom before we go home," she said.

"Now?" Ross said. "It's late. She's probably sleeping."

"It's not that far," she said. "I'll feel better if I do."

"I suppose it's a good night for a brisk walk," he said.

Mill fires roared, and the sky reflected orange. The air tasted of iron and smoke. When they exited the trolley, Ray ran ahead, reaching the house first. Violet and Ginny lagged.

"I win," he said. He took the front steps two at a time and left the door open.

"You raised in a barn or what?" Violet complained as she mounted the steps.

"Ginny and I will wait out here," Ross said.

"I won't be long."

Dread crept along Agnes's spine as she climbed the stairs and entered the house.

"Dad?"

"He's upstairs," Ray called from the kitchen.

Agnes took a deep breath and continued up the steps. Mom's breathing sounded worse. Agnes entered the room. Dad was asleep in the chair next to the bed. Mom looked pale.

"Dad," Agnes said. "Wake up."

"Huh."

"Wake up."

"What is it?"

"Mom doesn't sound good," she said. "I think you'd better call a doctor."

"Who?"

"I don't know," she said. "I'll get the directory."

* * *

The doctor took one look at Annie and told them to get her to St. Elizabeth Hospital in Youngstown. Her thyroid condition had weakened her, and she had pneumonia. She needed respiratory care. Agnes had Ross call one of the railroad men to borrow a panel truck. It arrived a few minutes later and parked in front of the house. Ross helped Dad carry Mom down the steps to the porch. Agnes followed with blankets.

"Is she going to be okay?" Violet asked.

"Of course," Agnes said. She rushed ahead, opened the rusting back gate, and laid the blankets in the bed of the truck.

"Careful," Dad said. The men lifted her inside.

Agnes glanced at the tires. Not much tread. She prayed they wouldn't get a flat while they traveled the dark countryside between New Castle and Youngstown.

"I'll ride with her," Agnes said. "You can ride up front." Dad looked relieved.

They drove through the darkness with Mom laying in the back, her head on Agnes's lap.

"It's going to be fine," Agnes told her, brushing back a curl from Mom's face. "They'll know what to do at the hospital." Annie grasped her hand and squeezed.

It seemed like it took hours to reach the new six-story light brick hospital. Mom wasn't breathing any easier after the long trip. They carried her up the central sidewalk to the front entrance. Agnes held the door while they moved Mom inside. A nurse greeted them and ordered a gurney. Mom was taken to a ward on the fourth floor that smelled of antiseptic.

Twelve beds lined the room, six on each side. Over half were filled. They transferred Mom to a spot near the door, two beds away from the nearest patient. That woman looked to be in her eighties, with white hair and skin so pale that Agnes could only tell she was alive by watching the blanket move above her chest. It was an hour before a doctor came in to examine Mom.

"There's no medicine for pneumonia," a bald doctor with thick glasses told them. "We'll keep her comfortable and do the best we can. She'll have to fight it off on her own."

Agnes heard the doctor's words but was more concerned with what she sensed in the dimly lit room. Spirits were like wisps of fog in the corner of her eye, whispers just out of range of hearing. At first, she assumed they were there for the old woman, to guide her to the spirit world when she passed. But after Dad and Ross left to find the cafeteria for coffee, Agnes felt them next to Mom's bed.

"She's not ready yet," Agnes whispered.

A spirit hand touched her shoulder.

"I know," Agnes said. "But she has not lived a full life." Mom wasn't even fifty. She was too young to die.

Dad and Ross returned looking glum. "The cafeteria wasn't open," Ross said.

"Why don't you two go home?" Dad said. "I'll stay with her."

"You can't stay alone," Agnes said.

"Someone needs to watch the young ones." Dad slid a chair to the side of the bed and sat down. "As much as I love them, two teenagers should not be overseeing the house."

Agnes nodded.

"Go on," Dad said. "It's almost midnight."

"You'll be all right?"

"Of course," he said. "I'll find a telephone in the morning and call."

Agnes glanced about the room. The spirits had backed away, but she didn't think they would be gone for long.

The roadway to New Castle followed the rolling countryside, sloping down to the Mahoning River bridge and back up again. A roadside stand was lined with pumpkins and straw bales reflected in the headlights.

Agnes had almost forgotten Halloween was a few days away. In Wales they built fires on the Vigil of Samhain. Each person would write his or her name on a white stone, which is then thrown in the fire. They would march around a fire, praying for good fortune. The next morning, they would sift through the ashes in search for their stones. If a stone was missing, it meant that the spirits would call upon the soul of that person during the coming year. They hadn't followed the tradition since they arrived in America. Halloween was for collecting candy, not interfacing with the spirit world.

Ross dropped her off at the house and left to return the truck. She found the girls already asleep in Violet's room. Raymond was reading in the parlor.

"How's Mom?" he asked.

"I don't know."

"Has Dad tried a healing?"

Agnes nodded.

"The spirits are around her, aren't they?"

Agnes took a deep breath.

"I'll be praying."

Agnes removed her coat and cleaned out the tea pot to make a fresh batch. She hadn't finished half a cup when she lay her head on the table and fell asleep.

She dreamed that she and Mom were strolling across a flower-covered meadow. "Watch for the fey," Mom said. "They will run circles around you. Then you'll be caught in their ring."

"It's almost Halloween," Agnes said. "We have to carve the pumpkins."

"You need to do that without me."

"I can't."

"The torch is passed." Mom smiled.

Agnes woke with a start, still sitting in the kitchen chair. The phone was ringing. She didn't want to answer it but forced herself to stand and lift the receiver of the wall phone. The hall clock said 5:15.

"Hello," she said.

"It's done," Dad said. "Your mom has passed."

The next week was filled with grief and prayers. They held the funeral at Ross and Agnes's apartment. Reverend W. G.

Wind traveled from Buffalo to take charge of the services. Lydia Marquette and her husband, Edward, were the first mourners to arrive. Lydia hugged Agnes tightly. "This is a loss for us all," she said. "But Annie will always be with us."

Agnes nodded, trying to keep her sadness at bay.

"If you need anything, call me."

"Thank you," Agnes said. She remembered the first day Lydia came to their house. She'd been canning tomatoes with Mom. That's when the idea of forming a Spiritualist church in New Castle was first proposed. Now there was the First Spiritualist Church, Spiritualist Church of Truth, and First Spiritualist Alliance. A new church, St. Elizabeth's Spiritualist, headed by Reverend Gantlin, was the first black Spiritualist church in the area.

Life goes on, she thought. But she didn't want it to go on without Mom.

CHAPTER 32

OCTOBER 2007: THE CART BEFORE THE HORSE

Karen stood outside the little church waiting for Rod to get out of the truck. The air was warm for October and the trees had begun to turn gold and red. Two large maples along the parking lot edge were totally yellow. There were five other cars already there. So much for the idea that she would be the only one to bid on the place. If it's meant to be it will be, she told herself.

Ron arrived in his construction truck. He was a stalky man with dark brown hair and clean-shaven face, not as tall as Rod. Karen felt less nervous with him being there. He had been to auctions before and knew what to do. $20,000 max. She had discussed the purchase price with Rod. That would be her limit. If they went much higher, they wouldn't have the money to do all the renovation they planned. Rod had a list of everything that needed done: new furnace, water heater, bathroom plumbing and fixtures, kitchen installation, dry wall, flooring. Even if he did most of the work, it was still going to cost them.

"Are you ready?" Ron asked.

"Let's do it," Karen said. She followed him in the side door and into the sanctuary.

Rod sat in the back while Karen and Ron moved to the front and sat in the first pew. There were about a dozen people there, including the minister. An older man paced around the room with a clipboard. At first, she thought he was the auctioneer, but as she listened to him talking with some other men, she realized he was a buyer, and by the sounds he'd already planned on getting the place.

When the auctioneer arrived, Karen was a nervous wreck. What was she doing here? She wasn't even an official Spiritualist minister and she was buying a church. Why had she listened to Janet? This better be what the spirits wanted.

The auctioneer opened the bid for $10,000. Here we go, she thought. It was too late to turn back now.

"Take your time," Ron said. "Don't bid any more than $500 at a time."

Karen took a deep breath and raised her hand. $10,500. The man with the clipboard scowled at her every time she made a counter bid. $12,000. $15,500. $19,000. "Twenty thousand," she called out. This was it. The do-or-die moment. If she was supposed to have the church, the man would back down.

"Twenty thousand five," he said.

Oh no, Karen thought. She should stop. He was over her price point. She glanced around the sanctuary. Were the spirits waiting for her to make another bid? It was the perfect place.

"Twenty and five going once."

"Twenty and five going twice."

"Twenty-one!" Karen shouted. What had she done? She didn't dare look back at Rod.

"Twenty-one," the auctioneer said. "Going once."

The clipboard man's face reddened.

"Going twice."

"Sold!"

The clipboard man got up and stormed out of the sanctuary.

Sold. What had just happened? She had just bought a church. It was hers. She was elated and terrified at the same time.

"I thought you were going to get carried away there," Ron said.

"I know," Karen said. "I said I wouldn't go past $20,000. I don't know what happened."

Rod joined them at the front of the church. "Well," he said, "it looks like I've got plenty of work to do."

"I'm sorry," Karen said. "I didn't mean to go over the price we set."

"What's a thousand dollars here or there?"

Karen looked around the sanctuary. So much work needed to be done. How was this ever going to become a real church?

* * *

Karen called Janet the next day to let her know she'd purchased the building.

"That's good," Janet said. "Now you can attend my mediumship program and be officially ordained."

Janet was right. She needed real training if she was going to be a minister.

The next two years became a constant cycle of going to work, remodeling the church, and finishing as much of Janet's class as she could from New Castle.

Rod started the remodeling project in the church basement. He gutted everything, old plumbing, electrical writing, drywall, and started to rebuild from scratch. They had a pebble-epoxy floor installed to hold out the dampness, created a new bathroom, and built a kitchen with commercial appliances. After that, came two furnaces, so they could heat the basement and sanctuary independently. That would save on heating bills. Karen didn't want to think what all of this was costing.

Rod didn't complain, at least, not too much. He probably liked the challenge of refurbishing the old building, but he was working full-time too. She hoped it wasn't too much for him.

Karen finished her spiritual study homework in the evenings and on weekends. Janet's assistant, Reverend Carol, sent her assignments. She had philosophy readings, and had to learn about conducting marriage, as well as naming and burial services. The largest commitment was a term paper on comparative religions. It seemed to take forever, but she finally finished it in November of 2009. Janet offered to ordain her at the New Castle church, but Karen wasn't ready for that. She opted to drive to New Jersey instead.

The Sunday of the ordainment services, Karen paused on her way into the church with Marilyn. The parking lot was full. She expected a lot of people, but now that the day had arrived, she was nervous.

"We should have done this in New Castle," she said. "There wouldn't have been such a crowd."

"Yeah," Marilyn said. "But then you would have had to invite your family and friends."

"What if I can't do the reading?" She told Janet she was only going to do one reading. Even that would be a challenge in front of a crowd of strangers.

"You'll do it," Marilyn said.

"I hope you're right."

Karen tried to relax during the service, but she couldn't. Janet spoke of turning herself over to the spirit world. Karen wanted to do that. She wanted to be of service. She wanted to help others. She just didn't want to have to get up in front of the crowd and demonstrate her mediumship. She wondered how Leonard and Janet had become so used to dealing with public demonstrations. They never looked anxious.

Karen was called forward to receive her certificate of mediumship. This is it, she thought. She was official. The church renovations would be finished soon, and she would begin to work for the spirits. Janet invited her to do a reading for the audience. Karen placed her certificate on her chair and took a deep breath. Please help me, she thought.

Jimmy. The name was clear.

"I have a Jimmy here with me," she said. "Can anyone take a Jimmy."

Three people raised their hands. Okay. She had to figure out which Jimmy she had. Her lungs felt constricted. "He died from a disease of the lungs. He wasn't very old, maybe fifties."

Two of the hands went down. She focused on a middle-aged woman with short hair and wire-framed glasses. "Brother?" she said.

"Brother-in-law," the woman said.

"Okay," Karen rubbed her palms together. I need to see more, she told the spirit.

The room faded from view and she saw the man riding in a large pick-up truck. Out the truck window, farm fields stretched to a distant tree line.

"Jimmy was a farmer," she said.

"Yes," the woman answered.

"He was a hard worker. I see big, calloused hands."

"Yes," the woman said.

"He wasn't much of a talker," Karen said.

"That's true."

"He wishes he would have told people how he appreciated them." Karen breathed deeply. "He sends much love to his brother and family. Please tell them that."

The woman thanked her.

The reading was over. Karen grabbed her certificate and returned to her seat, letting others take their turn. She hadn't made a fool of herself. Janet said a few more words and the service ended. Karen couldn't believe it. She was now Reverend Karen Heasley. She promised the spirits she would dedicate the rest of her life to them. And she would practice public demonstrations, no matter how difficult they were for her.

CHAPTER 33

A VISIT FROM BEYOND

While Rod finished remodeling the church's basement, Karen worked on obtaining a nonprofit status for the church and finding people to make up the board of directors. It took months to get the people and the paperwork organized. She must have been crazy to think this was going to work. Her lawyer didn't even know what Spiritualism was.

Rod erected a new sign in front of the building. It was kelly green highlighted by a logo Marilyn had created, a stone path leading through a forest to a bright light, gracing the top. Beneath it read: *Spiritual Path Church*, Reverend Karen Heasley. On the outside it looked like a real church. It was going to take some time to complete the sanctuary, but they could use the room as it was for a while. At least they had most of the original pews and a dais that had been left behind.

Karen decided to start small. She offered Sunday services at 11:00 am and Thursday evening meditation. She couldn't afford advertising, so she depended on word of mouth to bring people to the church. The meditation class attracted about a dozen people. Karen invited the attendees to come to Sunday services, but on their first Sunday, nobody showed up.

"I thought at least a couple of people would come," Karen said. Marilyn had spent hours preparing her sermon.

"It's going to take time." Marilyn shrugged. "We knew this wasn't going to be easy."

"I know, but I hoped we'd get someone."

"Well, look at it this way. My sermon is all ready for next week."

Karen wished she could accept things as easily as Marilyn. She'd completed all her studies with Leonard and Janet, and Marilyn had been taking classes in healing and spiritual art. All that work, and there they stood, alone in the sanctuary. What did the spirits want her to do now? She'd bought a church and invited people to come. And they didn't.

* * *

It had been four years since Agnes's mother's passing. Agnes hesitated to officially take her place. Raymond was a good medium, but his interest was in courting a local girl, Alice Covert. He didn't want the responsibility of caring for the church. Finally, in November of 1930, she decided it was time to be ordained. The weather was cold, but there was no snow to prevent Dr. Richardson from traveling from Buffalo, New York, where he was pastor of the First National Spiritualist Church. He arrived early in the day and had time to relax before the event.

Dad and Raymond took charge of the service, making sure the hall was decorated with flowers for the occasion. Agnes chose her best dress, a pea-green satin gown. Ross surprised her with a corsage of tea roses and lilies before she left for the event.

"You look lovely," he said.

"I don't know why I'm nervous," she said. "I've been a practicing medium for years."

"It will be over before you know it," he said. "Then you can give your dad some well-earned rest."

"The mill work had taken a toll on him," she said. Dad was thin but wiry. He would probably outlive them all. Mom would have to wait years to see him arrive in the spirit world.

The hall was almost full when they arrived with Ginny. Miss Bliss, Mrs. Veller, Miss Banister, Mr. Hughes. Mrs. Frameleiter and Reverend Mrs. Monday had come from Youngstown and were seated near the front. Agnes was surprised to see that Mrs. Becker and Mr. Penninggraft had traveled all the way from Erie.

"Good evening," Daniel Johns said from the dais. "Welcome to the Spiritualist Church of the Truth. Would you please be seated?"

The program began with a solo given by David Lewis, followed by a piano and violin selection by Miss Nellie Ingram and Raymond. After Dr. Richardson addressed the audience, he first awarded Margaret Davis with her first papers in licensed mediumship. They concluded the event with Agnes's ordination ceremony. As she was presented with a gold Spiritualist brooch and bouquet of flowers, she smelled Mom's favorite perfume.

* * *

Sometimes Karen would lay on the church pews and talk to the spirits, trying to reassure herself that she was on the right path. A spirit who said his name was John Edmonds came to her one day. He wore wire-frame glasses on his big nose and was dressed in a three-piece suit with an old-fashioned ascot instead of a tie.

"We all endure trials," he said. "This will be worth your efforts."

Curious about who the spirit might be, she looked up his name on the internet. Edmonds was a trial lawyer and judge who lived in the 1800s. He first published his experiences with Spiritualism in 1853, in the New York *Courier*. In the article he confessed to his complete conversion to Spiritualism. A furious controversy arose. He was pressured to resign his position on the New York Supreme Court because of his beliefs. Karen wouldn't have to go through that sort of trial, but opening a church that had no parishioners might be worse.

The following week Karen reminded her meditation class members about Sunday services. Again, no one came. And the week after that. And the next week. She and Marilyn waited fifteen minutes before turning off the lights and locking the doors. Finally, they had one woman show up from Ohio. A couple of others attended sporadically, but she had no real congregation. Karen was not a patient person, but even Marilyn, who had the patience of a saint, grew weary.

One day in March while Karen was out working in the church yard, a car drove by slowly. The woman stopped near the drive. Finally, she thought, someone interested in the church.

"Can I help you?" Karen said.

"Do you read the Bible in this church?" the woman asked.

"What?"

"Do you read the Bible?" The woman looked her up and down. Karen felt her stomach turn. This was what she was afraid of, that fundamentalist Christians would discover and target the church. Her worse fears were being realized. New Castle wasn't the place for a Spiritualist church. Why had she thought otherwise?

"This is a house of God," Karen said. "We believe in God."

The woman grimaced. She rolled up her window and drove off. It took Karen the rest of the day to shake the dread. She made sure the doors were locked when she was there alone. At meditation that week, she was still worried about the woman.

"What's the matter?" Marilyn asked before class.

Karen told her about the encounter.

"You knew some people weren't going to be happy about this place," Marilyn said.

"I know," Karen said. "But what if someone tries to burn it down?"

"I don't think that's going to happen."

"I hope you're right." Karen walked into the sanctuary and turned on the lights. They'd taken the dark paneling down, but the place was still dingy. "I wish I'd get some sort of sign that I'm on the right path."

That evening, women from the meditation group arrived promptly and joined together to increase the positive vibrations of the building. Karen closed her eyes and tried to stay positive, but her mind kept wandering. Poor Rod had been working so hard to make the church look bright and new. What if this was all a waste of time?

When the meditation ended, Karen again invited the class to attend Sunday services. She received the usual nods and I'll-think-about-its. That's when she heard the fluttering sound. At first, she thought it was the furnace, but it was too warm, and the furnace hadn't run all day.

A bird flew the length of the sanctuary.

"What's that?" one of the women called out.

"It's a bird!"

Another bird flew by. They both vanished through the wall. The class erupted in conversation. Karen and Marilyn checked the ceiling for holes. Nothing. There were no birds to be found.

"I think that was your sign," Marilyn said.

Karen nodded. "I hope you're right."

* * *

Agnes waited for Ross to finish counting the money in the donation basket. Evening light reflected off his hair, accentuating the gray. She hadn't thought much about getting old, not when her mother died young, not when her dad died in 1954. She was here to live life. Her purpose was to connect people with their loved ones who had passed. Life and death were a continuum to her. At least that's how she felt until Mabel died in March. It was 1957. Mabel was only sixty-two years old.

"Are you ready to go?" Ross asked.

"Yes." She followed him from the room, and he locked the door behind them.

Even though her mom's goal was to have a real church building, the hall had served them well over the years. She didn't want to admit it, but Spiritualism seemed to be waning. Change was all around. TV was taking the country by storm. *Ed Sullivan, Perry Mason,* and *Maverick* were the talk of the town. Elvis Presley was creating a big splash with his new rock-and-roll music. All the kids were playing with hula hoops. The Russians had even launched a satellite into space.

"Are you feeling okay?" Ross asked as they reached the foot of the stairs.

"Just a little tired." Ross had stood up for her and her beliefs to his friends and family and the community. She didn't think she could have taken over the church from Mom without him. But every month she officiated another funeral. There were few weddings. Soon, the congregation would be whittled down to nothing.

A week later, October rains blanketed the city. Agnes felt chilled to the bone and took to her bed. Ross watched over her, bringing her more blankets and hot soup, but her condition worsened. An ache spread across her chest and soon turned into a raspy cough. Finally, on Saturday, Ross took her to New Castle Hospital. He assured her she would be good as new in a couple of days.

Agnes smiled but she didn't dare mention to him that she was seeing spirits all around the room, including Mom, Dad, and Mabel. Even the babies, Cassie and Elsie May, were there. Agnes might be leaving the hospital soon, but she wasn't going home. She was going beyond.

Agnes Johns Guthire died on a Monday evening, October 21, 1957, just as the sun set in the western sky.

* * *

Once she retired in 2011, Karen focused on the church. It was make-or-break time. There were about ten regular parishioners by then. One woman drove from Ohio every week. Karen was happy to be asked to hold funeral services for a man she knew. She hadn't helped him pass on to the spirit world, but she at least was able to use some of her training.

In May, Janet called her. "How are things going at the church?"

"Slow," Karen said. This wasn't New Jersey. She wasn't going to get Catholics and Presbyterians to change their religions, and there weren't many people interested in spiritual beliefs, especially Spiritualism.

"I was thinking of coming over to bless the church and give you your spirit name," Janet said. "Are you busy over Memorial Day weekend?"

"No," Karen said. "That will be perfect. I'll make arrangements."

Janet arrived with Carol and Sharon on the Friday before

the holiday. They stayed at the Comfort Inn in town. Karen and Marilyn drove them up to Amish country the next day. Karen was used to seeing horse and buggies on the road in town, or Amish men working on house roofs. Many people she knew employed the Amish for construction. She couldn't understand why they were such a tourist attraction, but the women enjoyed seeing them.

The village of Volant sits in the middle of Amish County with its quaint shops, restaurants, wineries, and a distillery. They stopped in town and walked along the old-fashioned main street nestled between the hills. The focal point of the town was the mill built in 1812 along the bank of Neshannock Creek. The ladies spent most of their time looking at the primitive furniture, vintage kitchenware, artwork, and linens.

Karen was glad they enjoyed the outing, but at the back of her mind she worried. She'd invited several friends and her meditation class to the church blessing on Sunday morning. She expected a dozen people, twenty at most. It was embarrassing to admit to Janet that many Sundays there were still no people in the pews.

After a day of sightseeing and entertaining, Karen arrived home after dinner exhausted. Rod sat in front of the TV relaxing, but she was too nervous to completely unwind. Instead of sitting, she looked through her closet for an outfit for Sunday. What did one wear to a blessing and naming? She didn't want to be too fancy. Something professional and a bit dressy, she thought.

As the evening wore on, she heated water for a cup of tea. Some nice green mint might calm her down, but she didn't expect to be able to sleep that night. As she waited for the tea bag to steep, she thought she felt a light draft of fresh spring air, like a window had been opened.

Agnes. The spirit's name came to her, crisp and clear.

Hello, she said in her mind.

Nothing.

Hello? Agnes?

No answer. Karen was puzzled. The only Agnes she knew was a great-aunt. She didn't know why her aunt would visit.

Unlike Obie, she had no interest in spirits or fairies. It must be another Agnes. But who? And why would she visit now?

After a night of fitful sleep, Karen arrived at the church early. As she waited for Janet to arrive, cars began to turn into the gravel parking lot. Karen didn't recognize any of the people.

"Hello," Karen greeted the first group of women. "Welcome to the Spiritual Path Church."

"Hello," a younger woman said. "You must be Reverend Karen. Janet's told us all about you. We are so happy to be here."

She showed them into the unfinished sanctuary. "We still have a lot of work to do in here," she said.

"It's a lovely little church."

Karen soon discovered that Janet had spread word of the ceremony far and wide. People came from Youngstown and Pittsburgh. A total of one hundred seventeen showed up for the service. The room was packed.

Even though the air conditioning wasn't working right, no one complained. They began with a regular service. Janet blessed the whole building. Then they ate a catered meal in the finished basement. Janet held a book signing. Karen was dumbfounded. This was the way she imagined her church would be—filled with people enjoying a day of fellowship.

After the crowd had cleared, she and Sharon helped Janet pack the car. Karen thought of Agnes again.

"I had a spirit named Agnes come to me last night," she said. "Is she someone you might know?"

"No," Janet said. "I can't think of anyone by that name. What did she say?"

"Nothing," Karen said. "She was just there for a moment. Like a breath of fresh air."

Janet nodded.

"Maybe she came for the blessing too," Sharon said.

"Maybe," Karen said. "Maybe I'll discover who she is later."

Karen felt more confident after the blessing and began to reach out to others. She met Janet Decker at a psychic fair in Monaca, Pennsylvania. Janet told her about Temple Heights Spiritualist Camp in Maine. She and Marilyn signed up to do readings and healings for a week in July. When they attended an event given by Buddhist monks at the Ginger Hill Unitarian Church in Slippery Rock, Karen saved their names and contact information. She called to invite the monks of the Gaden Shartse Cultural Center to visit the church. They came to visit in November 2011 and attracted large crowds.

Since then, the church welcomed the monks back several times. Dr. Raymond Moody discussed near-death experiences in 2014. Dustin Pari of *Ghost Hunters* fame delivered an uplifting talk. Mediums from Lily Dale were guests at Sunday services. Spiritualists from England visited. Encouraged, Karen began broadcasting *Blogtalk* radio interviews and published a weekly blog covering a variety of topics. She finally felt like she had a real church.

AFTERWORD

When I moved to New Castle, Pennsylvania, I was interested in finding like-minded people. I discovered a yoga class downtown and joined a reading group at the library. I tutored at the local college and became involved with New Visions, a group interested in promoting the downtown.

I was attracted to New Castle because of the homes in the historic district, and live in an 1890s Victorian, so it was natural for me to visit the Lawrence County Historical Society. That led to a lengthy project, researching the history of the homes on the North Hill and publishing booklets about them. Before I knew it, I was working at the society as assistant administrator.

In September of 2012, friends invited me to a Murder Mystery Dinner to benefit a small congregation at the Spiritual Path Church. I had been interested in meditation and psychic phenomena since I was a teen, but I didn't know anything about Spiritualism. That night I enjoyed the meal and the entertainment. I met Karen and Marilyn at the ticket table, but my focus was on the mystery that night. Little did I know that I would be the one to solve another mystery for Karen.

A couple of days after the dinner, I discovered that there were two photographs of members of a Spiritualist church in the historical society's collection. One appeared to memorialize an important event. Seven people posed around a table which held a certificate. At the base of the photo in white hand-lettering it said: Spiritual Church of Truth, July 18, 1921. I thought the photo might be of interest to Karen.

After hours of research, I identified the people in the photo.

Annie and Daniel Johns sat in the front with their two younger children. Agnes and Ross Guthrie stood behind them with Dr. Richardson, a Spiritualist from New York. I made a copy of the photo and presented it to Karen.

"There used to be another Spiritualist church in New Castle," I said. I told her the names of the people.

"Agnes?" she asked.

"Yes," I said. "Agnes is Annie and Daniel's daughter."

It was then that she told me the story of Agnes coming to the church blessing. Since then, I've become friends with Karen. Her ambition is to help the living by receiving messages from those who had passed on to the spirit world. To bring hope and peace. The old Spiritualists struggled to have their beliefs accepted. So did Karen. But I know, like Agnes, she will succeed.

ABOUT THE AUTHOR

Susan Urbanek Linville received a PhD in biology from the University of Dayton and has lectured as adjunct faculty. She has administrative experience as an assistant editor for a science journal, university outreach coordinator and museum assistant administrator. As a freelance writer, she has published short fiction, newspaper and magazine articles, non-fiction books, and was a script writer for Indiana University's A Moment of Science Podcast Series. She is currently writing a weekly blog for the Spiritual Path Church in New Castle, Pennsylvania where she lives with her husband and four cats.

Susan's non-fiction books include an African memoir, an Underground Railroad history and historical neighborhood booklets. She has recently delved into the history of Spiritualism and has co-published a general book on Spiritualism and a book on early seers, mediums, and Spiritualists.

If you liked this book, you might also like:

Application of Impossible Things
by Natalie Sudman
A Very Special Friend
by Dolores Cannon
Being In A Body
by Victoria Pendragon
Little Steps
by James Adams
The Hobo Diaries
by Holly Nadler
Like A River to the Sea
By Paul Fisher

For more information about any of the above titles, soon to be released titles, or other items in our catalog, write, phone or visit our website:
Ozark Mountain Publishing, LLC
PO Box 754, Huntsville, AR 72740
479-738-2348
www.ozarkmt.com

For more information about any of the titles published by Ozark Mountain Publishing, Inc., soon to be released titles, or other items in our catalog, write, phone or visit our website:

Ozark Mountain Publishing, Inc.

PO Box 754

Huntsville, AR 72740

479-738-2348/800-935-0045

www.ozarkmt.com

Other Books by Ozark Mountain Publishing, Inc.

For more information about any of the above titles, soon to be released titles,
or other items in our catalog, write, phone or visit our website:
PO Box 754, Huntsville, AR 72740|479-738-2348/800-935-0045|www.ozarkmt.com

Other Books by Ozark Mountain Publishing, Inc.

The Anne Dialogues
The Curators
Psycho Spiritual Healing
James Nussbaumer
And Then I Knew My Abundance
The Master of Everything
Mastering Your Own Spiritual Freedom
Living Your Dram, Not Someone Else's
Each of You
Sherry O'Brian
Peaks and Valley's
Gabrielle Orr
Akashic Records: One True Love
Let Miracles Happen
Nikki Pattillo
Children of the Stars
A Golden Compass
Victoria Pendragon
Sleep Magic
The Sleeping Phoenix
Being In A Body
Alexander Quinn
Starseeds What's It All About
Charmian Redwood
A New Earth Rising
Coming Home to Lemuria
Richard Rowe
Imagining the Unimaginable
Exploring the Divine Library
Garnet Schulhauser
Dancing on a Stamp
Dancing Forever with Spirit
Dance of Heavenly Bliss
Dance of Eternal Rapture
Dancing with Angels in Heaven
Manuella Stoerzer
Headless Chicken
Annie Stillwater Gray
Education of a Guardian Angel
The Dawn Book
Work of a Guardian Angel
Joys of a Guardian Angel

Blair Styra
Don't Change the Channel
Who Catharted
Natalie Sudman
Application of Impossible Things
L.R. Sumpter
Judy's Story
The Old is New
We Are the Creators
Artur Tradevosyan
Croton
Croton II
Jim Thomas
Tales from the Trance
Jolene and Jason Tierney
A Quest of Transcendence
Paul Travers
Dancing with the Mountains
Nicholas Vesey
Living the Life-Force
Dennis Wheatley/ Maria Wheatley
The Essential Dowsing Guide
Maria Wheatley
Druidic Soul Star Astrology
Sherry Wilde
The Forgotten Promise
Lyn Willmott
A Small Book of Comfort
Beyond all Boundaries Book 1
Beyond all Boundaries Book 2
Beyond all Boundaries Book 3
Stuart Wilson & Joanna Prentis
Atlantis and the New Consciousness
Beyond Limitations
The Essenes -Children of the Light
The Magdalene Version
Power of the Magdalene
Sally Wolf
Life of a Military Psychologist

For more information about any of the above titles, soon to be released titles,
or other items in our catalog, write, phone or visit our website:
PO Box 754, Huntsville, AR 72740|479-738-2348/800-935-0045|www.ozarkmt.com